Why *did* the Chicken Cross the Road?

Why *did* the Chicken Cross the Road?

AS TAUGHT AT THE SCHOOL OF HARD KNOCKS

And Compiled

FROM AUTHENTIC RECOLLECTIONS OF A CHILD OF FORTUNE (AND MISFORTUNE)

Together

WITH OTHER ENGAGING ESSAYS ON CURIOUS PHRASES AND ANTIQUE WORDS THAT LINGER ON IN OUR DAILY SPEECH FROM DAYS GONE BY LIKE OLD SCARS FROM INJURIES LONG FORGOTTEN

With

SUNDRY ANACHRONISMS, RUSTY OLD SAWS, AND SPLINTERS OF FOLK WISDOM, YANKED OUT WITH A DASH OF HUMOR, SYMPATHY AND HISTORY (ANCIENT AND MORE RECENT)

Including

THE NAMES OF VARIOUS INDIANA CREEKS, RIVERS, FERRIES AND A FEW EARLY SETTLERS THROWN IN FOR GOOD MEASURE

By L. L. L. Murdock

Featuring Breathtaking

Illustrations by T. T. Heidel

ISBN 978-0-6151-8874-4

Published 2007 by Murdock/Lulu Press.

To Susie, for all that … and for all those years …

Du hast die schoensten Augen, Maedchen, was willst du mehr?

Fyodor Dostoevksy

You have the most beautiful eyes, girl, what more do you want?

LARRY L.L. MURDOCK grew up in the tough and rough coal mining town of Linton, Indiana, in the 1940's and 1950's. He never quite recovered, despite six years as instructor in a German university, forty-some trips to Africa helping teach poor farmers how to store their harvested grain safe from weevils, plus sundry other adventures, which include piloting a 1928 open cockpit biplane. His memories, love of the past and fascination with our curious English tongue, are here stitched together into a quilt of joy, history and whimsy, with a dash of nostalgia embroidered in for added color.

THELMA T. HEIDEL grew up on a small dairy farm in Random Lake, Wisconsin and has dabbled in drawing all her life.

FOREWORD

When I first got acquainted with Larry Murdock, now a quarter century ago, I quickly learned that this internationally recognized entomology professor has a passion about science. Perhaps that's one of the reasons why he so loves challenges. Larry seems happiest when he is tackling something new such as creating insect-resistant cowpeas (black eyed peas to us) for African farmers, or ways to store their grain after harvest – even if it took him 20 years to do so. During these two decades pest management researcher Murdock made over 42 trips to Africa. With patience and persistence he brought together people from different disciplines, countries, and institutions to join in the effort. Today the project he started, which was designed to create an insect-resistant Bt cowpea, is well on its way to success. His cowpea storage work likewise is promising to help millions of Africans, thanks to $11 million in support from the Bill and Melinda Gates Foundation.

Larry's demanding research and travel schedule notwithstanding, he took on additional challenges, first that of becoming a scratch golfer, then earning his pilot's license and getting his own plane – a Beechcraft Bonanza. That wasn't enough of a challenge, however, so he acquired a vintage 1928 Travel Air, an open cockpit biplane, and had it rebuilt. That's the plane he and his equally adventurous wife Susie fly, both appropriately attired with helmets and goggles.

As our life-enriching friendship deepened I also learned that Larry was working on yet another challenge: that of producing a unique book. One by one over the years he shared with me his short essays as, in the early morning hours before work, he coaxed them from his computer. It is a collecion of those essays, vivid glimpses of pioneering American history coupled with his own experiences of 50 years ago, that Larry brings to the pages that follow. "Researching and writing them," he says, "is pure recreation, a fun means of putting perspective into one's life. Teaching and research are fine but there must also be life outside the laboratory and classroom."

Why do I find Larry's capsules of rural American history so vivid?

Two reasons.

First, be his stories factual or fanciful, they mirror my own experiences or those related to me by my elders. As a Hoosier farm boy born in 1917, thus having lived through most of the 20th century, I too experienced rural life under circumstances almost as modest as those Larry portrays. His anecdotes from his always venturesome youth in a coal mining town leave no doubt as to their authenticity.

Second, I enjoy Larry's charming and creative play on words. He exposes their folklore origins, multiple meanings, usages, and wisdom. In so doing he demonstrates that the English language is littered with words and phrases from the forgotten past. Anachronisms from the early 20th century and before have survived the agricultural revolution to have new and unintended uses in today's urban society.

Larry even calls on Aesop's fables to slip bits of his philosophy onto the written page. And, by exposing the origins and intended meanings of now commonly-used words and phrases Larry enables us to better understand our own history.

Larry's next challenge? He is drawing up plans for the flat-bottom boat he expects to build and float down the Wabash, Ohio, and Mississippi Rivers all the way to New Orleans – just as he tells us Abe Lincoln did.

Lowell S. Hardin

Professor Emeritus, Purdue University
November 16, 2007

CONTENTS

Page

PREFACE

It's not my habit to read prefaces so I scratch my head now that I am writing one. Am I a hypocrite, perhaps?

I don't have anything against prefaces, mind you; it's just that I am always in a hurry to plunge into a new book headfirst and fully clothed, dispensing with the preliminary niceties. I'm like the ravenous lumberjack who shoves aside the canapés and hors d'oeuvres and belly flops instead kerplop into the mashed potatoes and the roast. The lumberjack doesn't need an appetizer and I don't need a preface.

No (it dawns on me), I am actually not a hypocrite to write these things because I can amuse myself while writing them.

Writing can be fun, after all. It entertains – at least the writer himself – me. And there is a second benefit: by writing about something I can find out what I think about it – often I don't know till I have finished. Sometimes – I'm embarrassed to mention it – I delight myself with my own words. I realize that maybe I'm like a toddler who gets up from his potty to admire the poop he has produced, whereupon he sometimes, out of pride, toddles off to Mommy and Daddy to exhibit in his extended hand a sample of his achievement. Sometimes I fail at writing, of course – i.e., there's nothing in the bottom of the potty. Undaunted, I throw away my disappointment and drag out samples of the good stuff I produced earlier; this I give to my friends to read in the eager hope they will enjoy it.

That's the spirit in which was made the book that splays open here before your inquisitive eyes. That's also the next-to-last scatological allusion in the book, the last until the reader comes to "Till the Cows Come Home." Be it noted, by the way, the above poop incident was drawn from real life, not made up to shock the delicate reader. The proud purveyor of the poop was one Ian Murdock, who now, thirty years later, labors valiantly in the vineyards of computer science.

Someone once told me that a preface should say something useful about the book that follows, maybe tell how and why the author went to the trouble of writing it. It *was* a lot of trouble, I swear; not the writing of it, I mean, but the assembling of the text and formatting of it and checking the spelling and grammar and all that. Finding ways to make it more interesting than my mere words alone could do was a challenge, too.

Three beautiful women helped me with all that.

First, there's Jody Aleong Green. Jody pitches in like a trooper when there's something to be done. For some reason or other she attached her eyes and her considerable organizational skills to my book project.

Next there is Thelma Toletino Heidel. She is a gifted artist, which the reader can verify by flipping through the pages that follow. Her black-and-white sketches bring vivacity to the book that it would not otherwise have. David Heidel, Thelma's dad, helped out our noble cause by suggesting the cow topic.

The third of the lovelies to which I owe truckloads of thanks is my wife, Susie, a petite woman as neat and beautiful today as she was 40-some years ago when I married her (or, rather, she married me). She read every word of these essays, identified sentences that ran on overly long like children that strayed too far from home; she detected and yanked out cockleburs of confused thinking, helped me conjure up lists of words and phrases, and generally encouraged the whole kit and kaboodle. Without her these essays would be reposing in a drawer somewhere, waiting to be discarded when they rummage through my stuff after I kick the bucket.

Three other people encouraged this enterprise far more than they know. My friend Lowell Hardin, now 90 years old, read each of these essays, one by one, as they came from my printer. Age seems to have little effect on him except make him even smarter (which is hard to imagine) and still more caring. Lowell never failed to have an encouraging word for me. And in a conversation one day he told me he had a crow to pick with me – this led immediately to a discussion of crows and to the essay on that subject that follows. For twenty-five years now I have puzzled over this question: Why there aren't more men (and women) like this extraordinary human being?

Rich Luxton, who appears briefly as an actor in these pages, is an old (literally!) high school buddy who was so much smarter than I was (Rich was a National Merit Scholarship Semi-finalist even though he attended a small-time high school). I always admired (and envied) his wit and intelligence. We reestablished contact a couple of years ago after a hiatus of thirty years. Rich's kind words encouraged me to write, too.

And so did Vivian Zollinger, editor of Owen County [Indiana] History and Genealogy. Vivian published in her quarterly journal early versions of many of the essays gathered here. When I finished an essay I would always send her a copy – hoping to amuse her. Her replies were always a delight, and encouraged me to write on.

Thanks Susie, Jody, Thelma, Lowell, Vivian, and Rich. With friends like you, what more could a man want?

Larry Murdock

Why *did* the Chicken Cross the Road?

It is October, 1960, and the orange ball of the rising sun compels Ray Ham and me to squint as we roar eastward in his black Volkswagen Beetle. We just turned off Highway 59 south of Linton, Indiana, onto a dusty country road, and we are late. The gravel road down which we are now speeding is a shortcut to the village of Marco – a place we in those days contemptuously referred to as a wide spot in the road. Marco straddles Highway 67, which leads to Vincennes. That's where we are ultimately headed this morning, to Vincennes.

In Marco, we will collect our third rider, Elizabeth Wines. We are car-pooling, for good reasons; neither Liz nor I own cars, and gasoline costs a painful 31 cents per gallon. The three of us are students at Vincennes University (a community college), and we all have 8 o'clock classes. I have an English test to face, and I'm anxious not to be late.

My thoughts turn to Elizabeth, a slender 18 year old – the same age as Ray and me. She has a thin, beautiful face, and rich brown hair that edges toward auburn; it is long and it shines, she washes it every day, I think. Her eyes are crystal blue, the kind you can get lost in. She dresses well, too, and is intelligent and well-spoken. I think of her with a hint of longing as a lovely young fox. Regrettably, she has a serious boyfriend, so I don't have any real designs on her; I just like her and like to look at her. Truth is, I love beautiful things, and so I look forward to seeing her and watching her in harmless enjoyment – besides, she takes my mind off my impending exam.

As we hurtle along – late because we had to stop for gas – the gravel crunches under the wheels while the puny VW engine whines, and a long column of dust arches behind us like a rooster tail. As we top a low rise there is a farmhouse on the right. Scattered across the front yard is a bunch of white chickens doing what chickens always do, walking around stupidly, clucking and cackling, pecking for worms and bugs while continually watching one another in case one of them discovers something edible. As we barrel toward the house Ray, grimly gripping the wheel, keeps his foot on the accelerator.

Suddenly, for some inexplicable reason, that flock of chickens decides to visit the other side of the road. One of them runs for it, then another, soon there is a stream of them. As we near the house I watch in fascination as this torrent of poultry, necks outstretched, take long chicken strides across our path, lengthening them when they realize that a gigantic black chicken hawk is swooping down upon them. As they clear the road in the nick of time, a straggler, presumably the slowest-witted of the flock, decides she needs to be on the other side of the road too. Too late! As that tardy hen disappears under the curved hood of the Beetle, I hear over the roar of the road a squawk and a bump and then a ball of feathers rises up over the curving hood and smashes into the windshield, leaving a bloody streak mixed with tatters of down. I remember seeing, for a mere instant, the dull eyes of that unfortunate hen as she thumps into the windshield and is hurled into the air in the car's slipstream. Looking back, I see a ball of feathers in its death throes flailing and kicking there in the middle of the road behind us. I glance at Ray and see he has a big grin on his face. Soon Ray and I are both laughing – at the stupidity of chickens. The dash of the idiot chickens has spiced up an otherwise boring commute.

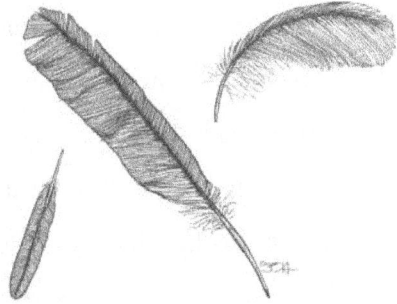

Did it ever occur to you, reader, that we humans hold chickens in substantial contempt? It's true, isn't it? Is it because they are birds and utterly stupid, bird-brained, one might say? Why, tell me, do we use chicken-related words when we make a disparaging remark about someone? Who hasn't said that someone is a dumb cluck? Come on! Is it fair? Deserved? I'm talking about the chickens, of course! Think of it this way: where would we be without chickens? No fried chicken dinner with gravy, no chicken and dumplings, no deviled eggs, no sunny-side up eggs, no eggs Benedict, no buffalo wings, no chicken livers, no chicken a la king, etc. You get the idea.

Yes, where would be we be without them, indeed? Without chickens, our American language would be as impoverished as our dinner table. My message here is simple, chickens deserve more respect! They've earned it!

This essay intends to strike a blow for chickens! Buc Buc Buc Buc Buc-uck!

When someone is running around wildly, directionless and out of control, we say he is running around like a chicken with its head cut off. This calls to mind my mother, a gentle soul who wouldn't deliberately hurt a fly. I mean it literally, not a fly. When one of those pesky flies was buzzing around our kitchen on a summer morning, she would shoo it toward the screen door and usher it outside instead of flailing away at it with a flyswatter. When there were too many of them for the shoo-fly maneuver, she handed me the flyswatter and set me to work as designated executioner – for which I was handsomely paid – a penny apiece. Mom never knew it, but when I badly needed money, I would furtively hold the screen door open to let in a few of them while Mom was out of the room – to increase my income.

In any case, Mom's reverence for fly-life didn't extend to chickens. From time to time we would return home from a Saturday visit to Grampa Burdsall's farm south of Lyons with an old hen trussed up on the floor of the car – for Sunday dinner. Converting that hen into fried chicken required that it be killed, a task Mom was adept at and had no compunction about doing. She would carry the trussed up squawking bird to the backyard after setting a kettle of water on the kitchen stove to boil. What happened next would make members of the Society for the Prevention of Cruelty to Animals cringe, or even weep. She untied the binder's twine from the hen's legs while holding its neck in her left hand (she was a lefty). Then, with a sudden rowing motion with her south paw she would pump the bird round and round, a very ungentle motion, what with the chicken's body rotating like a vertical hula hoop. At about the third cycle the head would pop off in Mom's hand and the unfortunate bundle of feathers would flop to the ground. What happened next I always watched with fascination though I had seen it a hundred times before: the headless bird would jump up and run crazily around, veering left and right while the featherless bloody stump of its neck spurted crimson streaks. Even at the age of six, I understood why the chicken ran around so erratically: without a head the poor thing obviously couldn't *see* where it was going. After a couple of dozen steps the headless bundle of feathers would collapse in a quivering heap, its legs kicking. Then, after a moment, it would stiffen and relax. Mom would then fetch the teakettle from the kitchen and douse the hen with boiling water. After plucking off the feathers and pulling out the entrails (which were thrown into the ditch in the alley behind the house), Mom would slice the chicken into the appropriate parts, and put them in a crock of water to cool in the icebox. (It occurs to me that my childhood was a lot more interesting than that of my grandchildren, whose chicken usually comes from the Kentucky Fried Chicken place.)

I confess I never learned how to wring a chicken's neck – though Mom often threatened to wring *my* neck; the reader will appreciate why I took her threat fairly seriously.

I wish I *had* learned to wring a chicken's neck – a nearly lost art, today, I suspect. I once needed that skill, and for lack of it I nearly lost the love of my life, my wife, Susie. I was her aspiring boyfriend at the time, back in the early '60's, and I was still trying to prove myself a worthy and a likely lad – to her mother, that is – not to Susie because by then Susie was already convinced that I was a Knight in Shining Armor. I knew she was a smart girl – after all she had taken a liking to me – but her mother was another proposition entirely. I suspected Mrs. Calvert didn't like me much, for after all I was a city boy from Linton, Indiana, and therefore automatically untrustworthy. I should explain that the Calverts, Susie's family, lived on a farm north of Worthington, about 15 miles northward of Linton.

One summer Sunday in 1961 I had been invited to dinner at the Calvert house. I saw this as a signal that I was in good stead with Mother Calvert.

As my dark green '53 Chevy crunches to a stop in the gravel driveway beside the house, I spy Mrs. Calvert by the back door, waving at me.

We exchange greetings and pleasantries. This feeds my hope that the mistress of the house is taking a liking to me.

"What are we having for dinner" I ask, innocently.

Maybe I am imagining it, but a diabolical shadow flashes across her face as she answers.

"Fried chicken," she says.

She goes on to say that Clarence, Susie's father, hasn't come in yet, and so the chicken isn't ready for frying.

"Is there anything I can do?" I inquire sweetly. I want to ingratiate myself and so win points.

"Yes, there is."

"What might that be?"

"Kill the chicken," she smiles. "It's down there in the backyard, trussed up."

I sense that it gives her pleasure to share this slightly dismaying (to me) news. It dawns on me that I am being tested. The city boy, me (actually, I am a mere small town boy, not a city boy at all, but never mind) needs to prove himself worthy. I stand there reading Mrs. Calvert's mind: "Any young man who can't kill a defenseless chicken has no business hanging around a farm. And he certainly doesn't deserve a farmer's daughter, either!"

After coughing and stuttering a bit, I realize that a bold stance is essential.

"Why of course, Mrs. Calvert, I'll be delighted to do it!" (This is a black lie, of course, but by now the reader realizes that there was a lot at stake.)

"Well, then, while you wring its neck, I'll get the water borlin." (Mrs. Calvert did indeed have a peculiar way of saying "boiling," but I pretended not to notice.)

"But uh, uh, uh, I prefer to chop their heads off."

"Huh? Don't you know how to wring off a chicken's head?" she eyes me suspiciously, eyes narrowing. I suspected I was being tested, and failing!

"Of course I do," I bluster, "but I do prefer the hatchet. I find it's cleaner and quicker." (I'm lying again, of course. I don't want her to know that I've never killed a chicken before, unless running over one with my car counts.)

"Have it yer way!" she says. "There's a hatchet in the garage and you can use that stump down there in the yard fer a choppin' block."

Rummaging around in the garage, I eventually find an old hatchet with a suspiciously dull blade. It looks like it has been used to chop rocks. It's so old I wonder if it once belonged to George Washington. Feeling the edge with my fingers I figure that if I swing extra hard, the dullness won't make any difference – the force of the blow will be such that the chicken's head will be pinched off by brute force.

Moments later, after untying the bird's feet and grabbing its legs firmly in my left hand, I struggle to get the resisting chicken – which annoyingly keeps squawking and kicking – to lay its head flat on the stump. It keeps raising it and peering at me, obviously begging for mercy. A couple of times I am on the verge of delivering the fatal blow, but the writhing chicken ducks out of position again at the critical moment. Every time I raise my hatchet-filled hand the idiotic fowl squirms and raises its head and I am forced to try to maneuver it back into position again. Minutes pass at this frustrating work. I am beginning to sweat. Every effort fails to get the dang%^&*$#! bird to cooperate and stretch out her neck so I can chop off her head.

As I struggle with this chicken-from-hell it dawns on me that Mother Calvert will never ever be Mother-in-Law Calvert someday unless I get this consarned chicken's head separated from its body. I am getting desperate.

Finally, after a struggle that seems to last for hours, despairing that I'll ever get the job done, I note that the hen is tiring because she momentarily lays her neck on the chopping black. At that instant I let the hatchet fall with grunting effort. I swing so vigorously my blow would have removed a hog's head, let alone a chicken's.

Alas! I regret to say that my dull hatchet blade, having got out of position on the backswing, merely grazes the poor chicken's neck. It buries itself instead an inch deep in the wood of the stump.

As the hatchet whops into the wood there is an explosion of feathers accompanied by a wild squawk, flapping of wings and flailing of hen's legs. Surprised, I let go of my grip on the chicken's shanks. Seconds later I watch, astonished, as the chicken – its head held at a weird angle, sprints across the yard and leaps the board fence enclosing the yard. Standing there, defeated, with the hatchet in my hand I am dismayed to see the bird disappear into the tall weeds in the woodlot surrounding the house.

"Oh, Man! There goes my dinner! How am I going to explain this?" An even more depressing thought follows: "There goes my lovely Susie, too, my maybe future wife!" Mother Calvert won't bear having an incompetent dunce like me – who can't even kill a chicken – for a son-in-law.

After puzzling over my dilemma, on the brink of despondence, I finally think of a way to rescue my dignity – and my dinner – as well as my potential future with Susie. I march into the house, stop before the gun rack, and take down the .22 rifle. I next stride bravely into the woods and shoot the chicken, which, in the meantime, has found her way to a high branch of a downed tree.

We had chicken dinner that day, after all, but I took a giant ribbing.

Letting Off Steam

I remember building a snowman a long time ago while giant flakes of snow drifted down around me like blobs of lost winter light. It was a magic hour, with the crunching snow and the jostling kids and the joy and laughter. That snowman eventually simply disappeared like snowmen always do, melting away on a dripping, warmer-than-usual winter day, with no one noticing. I didn't think of him for a long time after that, didn't think about the laughs and fun we had building him. But one day, months later, mowing the green grass on a warm afternoon in the spring, I stepped on a shriveled carrot that had once been his nose and bent over to pick up the two hunks of coal that had been his eyes.

Like that carrot and those bits of coal our English language is littered with words and phrases from the forgotten past. Those words and phrases nearly always reflect some long-outmoded technology that has disappeared from our daily lives. We hear, for example, almost every day, references to horses (horsing around, horse laugh, strong as a horse, changing horses in the middle of the stream, etc.), even though the four-legged steed (or sway-backed nag) has long-since disappeared from our streets. The same is true for words and phrases related to muzzle-loader guns, water mills, blacksmiths, and a great many other things. We often use quite peculiar words and phrases, which we recognize as strange only when, on rare occasions, we consciously think about what they mean and where they came from. Who hasn't been asked what they are doing "in this neck of the woods," a curious term indeed, if you think about it.

Many words and phrases we use today have something to do with steam, though few of us have ever seen or heard a real working steam engine.

Steam! The word once thrilled men (and women and children, too), made them go miles out of their way to gape and marvel at a steam engine at work. Steam was power, prodigious power, far beyond that of a mere horse or even a team of horses, power almost beyond imagining.

The nineteenth century was the very century of steam, thanks above all to the steam engine. It was the basis for countless labor-saving and time-saving applications that reached deeply into the lives of people in the cities and towns and hamlets as well as rural mid-western America. First there were the steamboats which, by the mid-nineteenth century, had caused flatboats, keelboats and canal boats to go the way of the falling leaves of autumn. The first steamboat to attempt to reach Indianapolis, Indiana, via the waters of the White River was the 52 ton Triton, out of Louisville, Kentucky. It was mid-May, 1828, when no one in my ancestors' home of Owen County, which was bisected by the White, had lived there more than a dozen years. We can imagine the hubbub the Triton caused among the citizens, young and old, to see that big boat pouring black smoke out her stacks, and backing and running and roaring to get over a bar or to shove past an overhanging tree. The Triton couldn't get over a riffle just north of Spencer, county seat of Owen, and was forced to drop back down the river. In 1831, the General Hanna did make it to Indianapolis, but the White proved forever too shallow and full of sand bars and riffles for regular steamboat traffic.

Close on the heels of the steamboat was the huffing, puffing steam locomotive, dragging passengers and freight at frightening speeds across the countryside, all the while pouring a volcano of sparks and soot out its billowing stacks. Oh, it was something to see and wonder at! The plaintive wail of a distant locomotive's steam whistle, now long gone, was as evocative of loneliness and longing as anything ever invented. The first railroad in Owen County, Indiana, was finished in 1854 by the New Albany and Salem Railroad Company. It passed from New Albany to Salem and on through Gosport and Crawfordsville to Michigan City, part of a grand scheme to connect the Ohio River with Lake Michigan.

Romantic as steamboats and steam locomotives were, steam had other, more mundane applications. There were steam-driven sawmills – a giant leap ahead from the old water-driven sawmills, which were regularly idled for weeks or even months when it didn't rain enough and the streams diminished to trickles. Steam-driven dynamos were the first sources of electricity in Owen County. In 1890, a steam dynamo was installed in Spencer, Indiana, to power the new-fangled (and wondrous!) carbon-arc street lights. Things like this were happening all over the United States in those days.

Coal mines had steam donkey winches that hauled miners' cages and mine-car loads of coal up from the bottom to the tipple. While the miners hewed away at the coal, steam-driven pumps carried water out of mines to keep them from flooding. In time, the hazardous deep mines of the Midwest were superseded by a new application of steam, the steam-shovel. With its big bucket and irresistible power it simply dug away the soil and rock from above the coal, laying it bare, thereby eliminating the need for dangerous burrowing into the earth to reach it. In the coal towns like my home town of Linton in Greene County, Indiana, steam whistles blew from every mine every evening, announcing by a code of long and short blasts whether the mine would work the following day. Every mine whistle had a special sound, and every miner knew the distinctive tone from his own mine. Among the miners listening were men who had reached the shores of America as immigrants from Poland, Scotland, or France. If they ever thought about it, they remembered coming to America – aboard a steamship. And the roads to the mine were built how? With the help of a steam roller.

Steam power reached the farm as well, with heavy, clumsy steam tractors plowing farmers' fields. Steam-driven threshing machines helped finish the harvest of grain, too. Such machinery had a negative side: it was so heavy it got bogged down easily in muddy fields. And taking a steam tractor from farm to farm meant driving it across rickety bridges built to carry mere horses and wagons; more than one ponderous behemoth went crashing through the boards and plunged down into the stream. Starting out from the farm, before collapsing the bridge, that tractor may have passed another steam-driven vehicle, the Stanley Steamer, which, for a time, contended with the gasoline-powered automobile to be king of the road.

Steam was even a villain at times, most notably when John Henry, the steel-drivin' man – driving steel to make a tunnel into a mountainside – competed against a steam drill. John Henry won, but died just as the contest ended, of exhaustion.

Music was made by steam, too, in the form of the steam calliope, invented in 1856 by Joshua C. Stoddard of Worcester, Massachusetts. An inventive guy, he loved train whistles. In a moment of inspiration he invented a device he called the steam piano, essentially a series of steam whistles played by a keyboard. Stoddard's novel musical instrument was – may I say – a resounding success – you could hear it

playing for miles when the wind was right. Soon every steamboat, county fair, and circus had its own steam calliope. But the story doesn't have a happy ending. Instead of becoming rich and famous – even though the steam calliope became very popular – Stoddard reaped only disappointment and scorn. His own parents were embarrassed that their son had invented something so useless. The next humiliation came when the town of Worcester banned playing the steam piano within the city limits. And Stoddard himself was pushed out of his own company within a few years; his enemies claimed he was a poor manager. Clearly, you had to be careful what you did with steam – you could get burned by it, as Stoddard proved.

With steam machines everywhere, in factories and mines, in amusement parks, on the river, on the streets of villages and town, on farmer's field, even rushing tooting through the countryside on iron rails, it's no wonder steam-related terms became part of our daily speech. And so, now, when we get good and started on a task, we say we are just getting up a head of steam – in other words, ready to really move forward on the job. When we plunge into a job with wild abandon despite the obstacles, it's full steam ahead. And which of us hasn't gotten all steamed up because someone didn't do his job right. For that matter, who hasn't had a boss who got so angry that steam was coming out of his ears? After a day of hard work at the job, people still congregate at the nearby bar to have a few drinks – to let off steam. Being hit by a steam roller is a way we still describe when we feel like we've been flattened by an irresistible force.

I think I'll end this essay now because I can't think of any more examples. I guess I've run out of steam.

A Memoir of Beans

Charlie Brock kept a vegetable garden on the vacant lot across the alley from our outhouse. His plot wasn't more than an eighth of an acre but it was still too much for him to spade up by himself. He was retired, an old man who had spent most of his adult life stooped over in a coal mine picking at the coal face or shoveling coal into mule-drawn cars. In that brutal work his back had once been broken by a slate fall; another time his hands were crushed against the top of the car. He said he could always tell when stormy weather was coming because his hands hurt. He grunted when he bent over, too, every time. I didn't understand that because I never grunted when I bent over. Of course I was only six years old or so and didn't understand such things.

In those days when Charlie and I hung out together – it was in the late 1940's and early 1950's – he was in his seventies. He had pale blue eyes and a full head of hair, grizzly gray, which Dellie, his wife, cropped once a month. She'd set him down in the yard on an old white-painted wooden lawn chair, throw a sheet over his shoulders, and whack away at him with her sewing scissors. Charlie and Dellie thought it was stupid to pay 50 cents for a haircut at Darwin Banks' barber shop downtown when you could cut it yourself for free. Yes, the couple was tight-fisted when it came to money, but that was because they had lost all theirs in the Depression when the Linton bank where they kept it failed. That was in '33. Since then they hid their life-savings in their house, handfuls of hundred dollar bills stuffed under the mattress. It didn't bother them that it didn't earn any interest. Lost interest was piddling compared to what they might lose if they put their money in a bank. Besides, they slept easier, it being in easy reach and all.

Charlie usually had two or three days of whiskery growth on his chin because he shaved just twice a week, on Saturday after his weekly bath, and on Wednesday before he went to town. He used a straight razor, which he stropped himself, and in the summer he shaved outside using a mirror hung on a tree, because the light was

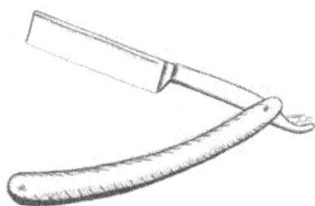

better than in the house. He wore long underwear, cotton in summer, wool in winter. I can see him standing by that box elder tree, his suspenders off his shoulders and hanging down to his knees

on either side, chin up, head cocked, scraping his whiskers off with the razor. It actually made a scraping sound.

It didn't help a lot when it came to spading gardens that all Charlie had for a helper was me, his main side-kick, a wide-eyed, snot-nosed boy. I'm pretty sure the old man enjoyed a companion, even one as insignificant as me. Maybe the fact that he never had a son had something to do with his tolerating me, I don't know. He had one daughter, who survived the diphtheria that killed her older sister back in '03, but she was grown up and married now.

Every morning in the summer (except on Sundays), I'd wake up, shovel down a bowl of Cheerios, and scamper off to Charlie's place two houses down Second Street. Usually I'd find him sitting in the swing in his screened-in porch facing F Street, smoking his morning King Edward cigar and thinking about what he was going to do today. One thing about Charlie, he was never in a hurry. Today, fifty or sixty years later, a never-in-a-hurry guy like him would be viewed as slightly cracked, an anachronism, like Rip Van Winkle wandering out of the mountains and back into Tarrytown. I suppose today's hurry-up attitude is progress of some kind or other. For sure, it's built on the idea that slow is bad and fast is good. Charlie (and I, as his sidekick) had carried our thinking far beyond that principle. We acted as if time meant nothing at all and so we never ever hurried, and there was simply no such thing as slow or fast or hurry. Of course Charlie never carried a watch and I didn't either – I couldn't tell time yet anyway, and so had no need of one. If, as rarely happened, Charlie really needed to know what time it was – as, for example when he ran out of cigars and needed to get some from Red Monier's store up on H Street, which closed at 5 o'clock – he'd look at the sun and tell the time with tolerable accuracy, good enough to know if the store had closed yet, anyway.

Garden-making time rolled around every year as sure as the geese came north in the spring, and so in the natural order of things Charlie would persuade some farmer from the edge of town to bring his horses to plow his little garden. When that fellow and his team came clip-clopping and jingling down the alley from H Street, it was something to see. They always came in the late afternoon when the shadows of the coal sheds and privies that lined the alley stretched all the way across it. Hearing the jingling and the clopping, people came out their back doors to watch. By then most farmers plowed using tractors already, but people still loved to see a team of horses at work, and came out to gawk.

The farmer had been plowing his own fields since early morning but brought his team at the end of his workday before he unhitched, eager for the easy five dollars Charlie promised him. Coming down the alley from H Street, he strode along behind his two chestnut mares harnessed up with big black collars and brown leather reins and shiny steel bits between their teeth. The big brutes themselves were held apart (but linked together, too) by a neck yoke and they were attached to the single-bottom plow by means of separate singletrees dangling over their big haunches. The reins passed from their mouth bits over their backs and then over the shoulder of the plowman. He steered the plow – which looked like a giant wooden wishbone with a two-foot long shiny steel plowshare at its tip. The plow itself was supported on a little wheeled carriage so it didn't dig into the roadway. Dressed in dusty denim overalls and a sweat-stained straw hat that looked like it had been sat upon more than once, he held on to the tips of the wishbone with sunburned hands and called to the horses, "Gee, Bessie!" or "Gee, Nellie!" "Giddy up!" He flicked the reins and called and the horses grunted and snorted across that little field with their harness leather squeaking and the metal linkages clinking. As they worked you could hear the sighing and plumping of the earth as it was sliced by the plow and then slid up the plowshare and tumbled over, plopping back to the ground like a wave of chocolate pudding in slow motion. It didn't take more than a few minutes to till that postage stamp of a garden.

A week or two later, after the rich brown-black ridges of soil had settled and been smoothed by a couple of good rains, it was time to plant. Potatoes and cabbage sets went in first, and then, later, turnips and carrots, and as the days lengthened and the soil warmed, the tomato seedlings and corn and parsnips found their places. Stakes and white kite string kept the rows straight and gave the field a pleasing geometry. Finally, the pole beans went in, the best part of a garden. I loved the pole beans as much as I hated the potatoes.

Pole beans need poles. For Charlie's garden we used willow saplings we cut ourselves over by one of the stripper ponds north of Linton High. One morning, while the sun beamed low in the east and the birds sang and the robins ran little sprints across the yard, stopping and cocking their heads to listen for worms, Charlie declared that it was time to go and cut some bean poles. Soon we were trudging up the alley, the old man Charlie with a hatchet dangling in his left hand and me, the kid, with my pockets stuffed with binder's twine to tie up the bunches of poles. Why didn't we take a car, you say? Because Charlie didn't own one. He didn't even know how to drive. He never got beyond driving a team of horses and a wagon. He said he didn't need to drive a car because he could walk anywhere he really needed to go.

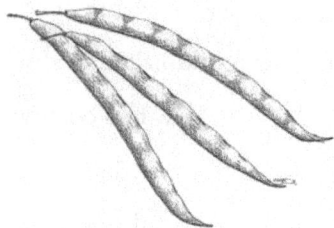

It wasn't more than a mile to Horseshoe Pond, but it took us the better part of an hour to get there. Why should we hurry? We had all day, and it was beautiful out, just warm enough that we weren't too hot or too cold. People then (at least old men and little boys) weren't yet trapped in the jaws of the notion that every minute is vital for getting more and more work done, i.e., that the only thing in the world that is important about a man (or a boy) is the amount of work he can pile up in a day. For Charlie and me, every minute counted too; but it counted because we liked to savor it, to look at it and smell it and feel it and lick it like an all-day sucker. Why should a person be in a hurry when there was something wonderful right there before his eyes? And goodness knows there certainly were things to enjoy everywhere, like the cardinal whistling in the mulberry tree or the red-winged blackbird that scolded and swooped at us when we walked too near her nest on our way out to the pond. We thought poor people were the only ones in a hurry, by which we meant the poor in spirit and impoverished in leisure. Rich people like Charlie and me had all the time in the world.

North of the baseball diamond, past the Grove – three or four acres of shagbark hickories and oaks set aside as a park years ago – we had to make our way across a muddy flat before we climbed up the bank of Horseshoe Pond. We crossed the low place by stepping on old boards someone had thrown down for that purpose. I scampered over, hopping and giggling, excited by the risk of stepping into mud over my shoes and by the challenge of avoiding it. Charlie, by contrast, was exceedingly deliberate. He tottered across using a broken limb as a crutch, stepping uncertainly from board to board with wobbly dignity. Moments later, at the top of the bank bordering the pond, we turned down the left-hand path made by fishermen, then, after a hundred steps, we descended through a thicket of green horsetails into the soggy marsh partially enclosed by Horseshoe's waters. (I am forced to interject here that Horseshoe was shaped more like a question mark than a horseshoe, a fact which I had noticed already when I was five years old. I was perplexed by this and troubled by it and wished to change it for the sake of accuracy, being then already a stickler for accuracy. But somebody else had given the pond its name long before, so what was I to do? If I referred to the pond as "Question Mark," people would look askance at me and wonder what I was talking about.) Clumps of willows were scattered here and there in the marshy ground, and we set to work. Charlie did the chopping, selecting one-inchers that were eight or nine feet long, and straight. My job was to

strip off the leaves and lay the poles in piles. Soon we had two bundles tied together with twine, one with sixteen and the other with eight poles. Minutes later Charlie and I, the old man and the boy, were trudging for home, the thick ends of our bundles over our shoulders, the narrow ends dragging the ground several feet behind us. We made our way slowly and with dignity, as proud as explorers returning from the ends of the earth.

The next morning early we were in Charlie's garden planting the beans. First, we heaped up a little pile of soil and poked in five or six seeds of Blue Lake or Kentucky Wonder. These two were his favorite varieties. If you asked him he'd wax poetic about their relative merits. I was in awe of him; he seemed to know so much about everything. In a square around the hill we stuck four poles into the ground, shoving them several inches into the soil to secure them, inclining them inwards so that they came together six or seven feet about the ground. We tied them together at this point with binder's twine. Of course I couldn't reach that high, so Charlie had to do it. The resulting frame looked all the world like a naked miniature teepee built with only four poles. When we were all done that corner of the garden looked like a little Indian village with six teepee frames.

Since beans are so much a part of our culture and have been part of it since about the time our ancestors stopped grunting and began to articulate our delicate thoughts with actual words, it's no surprise beans have worked their way deep into our language.

I remember a meal of Navy beans I once ate with Charlie and Dellie as clearly as if it happened an hour ago. Charlie and I sat at the square granite-topped table in their little kitchen while Dellie pulled an iron-ware pan of cornbread out of the oven of her wood-burning stove. That stove was a big black cast-iron monster with six burners. It burned wood in the fire box at the bottom, below the oven. On one of the burners there simmered a steaming pot of boiled beans. We split our cornbread muffins with our kitchen knives, smeared them with butter, and then marched, plate in hand to the stove, where we ladled on piles of steaming beans, getting maybe a hunk of fat-back bacon in the bargain. Back at the table we ate in silence, the only sound being the clink of our spoons on our ironware plates. Minutes passed. Eating at the Brock house was serious business, I knew. It was not the place for idle chatter but for the serious business of filling one's stomach. As we soaked up the last of the bean sauce with a hunk of crumbly cornbread on which we had spread some blackberry preserves, and settled back into our chairs, satisfied, it came: Charlie belched, loudly and contentedly. A moment or two later Dellie belched, as in reply. After a moment of silence, Charlie followed with a second belch, shorter than the first, but still emphatic. Dellie belched again. I watched, a little kid, fascinated. Over at our house you weren't supposed to belch, and if you did, you were required to promptly say "Excuse me!" There followed another round of belches. Like a fan watching a tennis match, I glanced back and forth at the two belchers when their turn came. After a while we all got up, leaving the dirty dishes on the table, and went out to the porch and sat in the swing. Charlie lighted his pipe while Dellie took up her Linton Daily Citizen – she always read every line in it, though she sometimes fell two or three days behind. Sitting out there with the old couple I remember being puzzled by their belching. Only now do I understand it. Charlie was saying, in his simple hill country way, "That was a good meal, Dellie." Dellie, using the same strange language, was replying "I couldn't agree with you

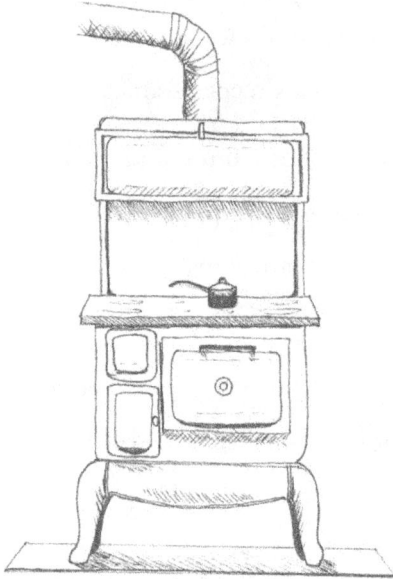

more." So Charlie responded with his next belch: "I really mean it, it was darned good." And so Dellie says "Why thank you, Dear, I know you appreciate it." And so it went: "You're a good woman, Dellie." "You're a good man, Charlie." Their belches spoke their thoughts better than mere words. Thus beans wove their way through the woof of my young life.

It occurs to me that bean terms, curiously, are almost always ones of negativity. When food-tasting experts say a dish has a beany flavor, it's not a term of praise, but disparagement. When some event or happening has no significance, it doesn't mean beans. And when somebody says I don't know beans from a hole in the ground, I know what he means (though I don't necessarily agree). Another way of saying the same thing is to claim that I don't know beans from apple butter – which is a high insult, considering how easy it is to tell the two apart. When a fellow says that something isn't worth a hill of beans, I understand that, too – one hill of beans isn't worth much, after all. To assert that a girl is as skinny as a bean pole was not to pay her a compliment back in the '50's, though it would be high praise these corpulent days when nobody is skinny. When we want to say that someone doesn't know what he is talking about, we say he is full of beans, in other words, he doesn't know beans about the subject. Someone who doesn't respond to a question has beans in his ears. In the good old days – actually, they weren't that good, in fact – more than one kid was taken to the doctor after stuffing a bean in his ear;

perhaps he was curious to know if it would fall out the other side when he shook his head. The nose was also occasionally a receptacle for beans, too. In either case the doctor always shook his head in disbelief. When a baseball pitcher aimed at your head, he threw a bean ball – in that case the bean in question was one's head. In case the reader is wondering, to compare one's head with a bean is not a compliment. An official personage who dabbles in the minutiae of management isn't an imaginative leader, he's a bean counter.

As kids we would buy little plastic pipes and blow beans at our playmates with them – bean shooters. And we built our own slingshots using the whittled off crotch we cut from a little tree, assembling the thing with strips of rubber sliced from old bicycle inner tubes and a leather patch cut from the tongue of an old shoe. We called these weapons bean flippers and shot them at sparrows (we called those birds spatzies for some obscure reason), or stray cats. Sometime when we had lost our ball, Mom would take some pillow ticking and make us bean bags to toss around.

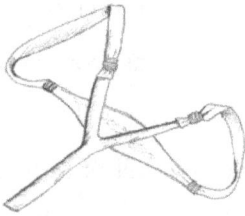

Maybe the trouble with beans is that they are so common, and cheap. Perhaps that's why they have worked their way so deep into every language and culture. Everybody knows, for example, the story of the magic beans in Jack and the Beanstalk. Destitute, Jack traded his mother's cow for a handful of beans. This seemed to be a dreadful mistake, and his mother was heartbroken. Thanks to planting those beans, though, Jack eventually acquired a goose that laid the golden eggs as well as a magic harp, and lived happily ever after, marrying a beautiful princess. In ancient Greece, elections were won or lost when the white beans in the voting urn were more numerous than the black beans. Everyone who has ever held them in their hands knows that Mexican jumping beans (which jump thanks to the insect larva living inside them) are like magic.

The real magic of beans, though, owes to their wonderful nutritional properties. Who doesn't know the sobriquet of Boston, namely "Beantown" thanks to the wonderful invention of Boston baked beans? Pork and beans is a delectable dish, as are shellie beans, beans and rice, refried beans, soup beans (served daily in the United States Senate dining room, by the way), three bean salad, chili beans, and bean casserole.

I'd better quit now before the reader declares me full of beans. My final thought is a slightly embarrassing ditty we recited when I was a kid:

> "Beans, beans, the musical fruit
> The more you eat the more you toot
> The more you toot the better you feel,
> So let's have beans for every meal!

Then there is another verse …..

> "Beans, beans, they're good for your heart,

The more you eat the more you ... (what was that word? – danged if I can remember.)

Since I seem to be rambling now I think I'm going to sit down and rest in my favorite place of relaxation – my bean bag chair.

A Million Bucks

At one time or another, all of us have felt like a million "bucks" – all too rarely, yes, but it has happened.

This curious term has an odd link to American pioneer history. The newly-opened lands on the sundown side of the Appalachians invaded by the ancestors of us Mid-westerners was once called simply the "Western Country." As the pioneers came in, they owned little except what they carried with them. Most of them were short – or entirely devoid – of cash money. The West in those days – from the Alleghenies to the Mississippi – was separated from the nearest mint by dozens of unbridged creeks and sundry big rivers as well as an ocean of uncharted woods. From necessity, our stalwart forefathers had to concoct some kind of currency to substitute for the scarce coins and the even rarer paper bank notes, many of the latter being of suspect value anyway. Our pioneer fathers eventually hit upon a solution to the currency problem, thanks to the abundance of game and their prowess as hunters: the buck skin. In 1810, at the Fort Wayne, Indiana, Trading Post, the value of a buck skin was noted to be exactly 100 cents. This was an amount already fixed by convention. Hence, a dollar was equivalent to a "buck."

It's true that the "buckskin" was too big to fit in a pioneer pocket, but it had inherent value. It was durable and could always be tanned and made into useful articles such as hunting shirts and leather pouches. It could also be traded between individuals, used to pay debts, taken to the general store and exchanged for cloth or gunpowder, or even sold for cash money in the larger towns.

No wonder all of us love to feel like a million bucks – unfortunately, most of us are forced to *imagine* what that feels like.

Indian-uh ....

ne of the more amusing quirks of history is that we owe the name of our State of Indiana to good old Christopher Columbus.

To his colossal mistake, that is.

Thinking (or hoping) he had discovered the Indies (China, Japan, India, etc.), that fabled land of spices, silk and splendor, he naturally named the first people he stumbled upon "Indians."

Late at night, when he tried to sleep, he was perhaps kept awake by the thought that the first "Indians" he had met were impoverished, naked wretches, people who carried primitive bows with arrows tipped by sharpened stones.

Where were the palaces with the golden roofs?

Something was wrong here, he must have realized.

But Columbus was a true believer, and never really doubted that he was at least *close* to the Indies. The man was, after all, a genius of inspiration, courage, imagination, and mustard-plaster stick-to-it-iveness, so he was undaunted by the fact that the natives weren't wearing silks and rubies. He was also the first great booster, spin-doctor, self-promoter, great-persuader, and showman. And so, during trips back to Spain from the "Indies," he brought along some of the Indians he had encountered, parading them before King Ferdinand

and Queen Isabella. Those miserable, undoubtedly bewildered showpieces, together with a few measly nuggets of gold, were exhibited as proof to his sponsors that Columbus had at least discovered *something*. Ferdinand must have looked at Isabella with a grimace.

Columbus hadn't discovered very much, it is true, but it was better than nothing.

The name "Indian" caught on. Columbus, clever fellow that he was, knew that if people in Europe accepted his name "Indian" this

would subtly reinforce the notion that he had in fact discovered the Indies. That would make him famous. Being famous would help him become rich. He wanted that, too.

Soon back in the Indies, he began rounding up Indians and selling them as slaves – an act which, recently, after 500 years of glory, has brought the outraged liberal world crashing down on the poor Italian Navigator's head. They paint him as a destroyer of native cultures, saliva dripping from his pointed European fangs, as a devastator of New World idyllic harmony. A hero when I was a child,

Christopher Columbus has in the meanwhile become a cultural pariah, a proper cell mate in the dungeon of history with Vlad the Impaler, Genghis Khan, and Adolph Hitler.

In any case the word "Indian" eventually became the common English name for the aboriginal people of America, malappropriately, of course, but history isn't fair.

A century after Columbus, when English colonies began to be planted on the east coast of North America, encounters with native peoples began to color American history. In Virginia and Massachusetts, "Red" men at first welcomed and helped the "White" men from Europe. You remember Squanto, from the Pilgrim days, don't you? Before long, though, things went sour, and these folks of different tints were eagerly killing one another – exactly the same thing that had happened with Columbus and the Indians down in the Caribbean back in the 1490's. It seems, due to some perversity on their part, the Indians didn't want to be made slaves, or give up their land. But the Europeans had guns (er … aquebuses and blunderbuses) for which stone-tipped spears and arrows were no match.

The predominant color of the times was red, thanks to all the spilled blood.

The Indians held all the land originally, of course, but the Europeans, especially the English and Dutch, came and found excuses to seize ownership of it. In time, the eastern seaboard became settled by Europeans, who, not surprisingly, hugged the shore and spent most of their time looking longingly east toward their parent countries – whence, they knew, came all good things.

Eventually, though, ambitious and prosperous colonial businessmen cooked up schemes to acquire still more land from the Indians. Most of that unclaimed land now lay west of the Alleghenies.

The Indiana Company, formed in 1763, sought to acquire undisputed ownership of a huge tract of land in present-day West Virginia. (Incidentally, a stock-holder of the fledgling company was one Benjamin Franklin.) The huge tract of western Virginia in question had been ceded by the Iroquois as compensation to some colonial traders who had been robbed (or so they claimed) at Indian hands.

The Indiana Company tried hard to get the official blessing of the British government for their acquisition. Without it, they owned nothing. Their pleading, hand-kissing and importuning in King George's Court dragged on for years. During those decades various other companies sprung up with the idea of getting rich in land, too. Among the earliest were the Ohio Company and the Vandalia Company. Like the Indiana Company, these two made their own moves to grab land in the Ohio River Valley.

Eventually, though, in 1798, the Indiana Company fizzled out, but the name survived. So, in 1800, when the Congress in Washington, D.C., divided the Old Northwest Territory into two parts, they named the western part "Indiana Territory." This took in everything in present-day Indiana, Illinois, Michigan, and Wisconsin. The remaining part, Ohio, was lopped off to become a state three years later.

The name "Indiana" seemed appropriate for the western part of the new Territory, because much of it was still roamed by Indians: Potawatomies, Wyandots, Kickapoos, Weas, Miamis, and Shawnees. These troubled peoples, who merely wished to live their traditional lives while still trading with the Whites, had long since been driven from their ancestral lands in the east and south. Alas, from Indiana Territory they were, in time, also driven out by land-hungry settlers and ambitious politicians.

The sad story of the slow extinction of the Indiana Indians lingers on in the names of battles and travails: Lochry's Defeat, the Pigeon Roost Massacre, Harmar's Defeat, St. Clair's Defeat, the Battle of Tippecanoe, and the Battle of Fallen Timbers. By 1840, the Indians were gone forever. One of the ironies of history is that Indiana has no official Indian tribes living within her borders.

But the Indians left other remains – their words and names – which lie upon the land like time-worn milestones inscribed in a forgotten language. The meanings of these names have mostly been lost to us, even though the names themselves are as familiar as the tree in the front yard.

There are names for geographical features like rivers or streams: Muscatatuck, Kickapoo, Patoka, Chippewanuck, Wea, Wabash, Mississinewa, Tippecanoe, Little Shawnee, Big Shawnee, Iroquois, Kankakee, Salamonie; or towns – Muncie, Peoria, Mishawaka, Modoc, Topeka, Mohawk, Blackhawk, Mongo, Delaware, Wawaka, Monoquet, Winamac, Majenica, Cayuga, Miami; or lakes – Shakamak, Muskelonge, Shipshewana, Manitou, Winona, Maxinkuckee.

Indian words have become part of our daily speech, too; often they describe objects or implements invented by the Indians which we adopted. Others describe natural things that were part of the Indians' world long before the White man came.

Everyone knows the meaning of the word canoe, of course, and has probably ridden in one. And most every man or woman has worn moccasins, even though he or she probably hasn't ever walked a mile in those of another person. Nearly everybody can tell the difference between a catalpa and a sycamore, both of which are Indian names for common Indiana trees. If you don't know the difference between a skunk, an opossum and a moose, you're in trouble, but you will be excused for not knowing they are all Indian names. If you have ever lain in a hammock and smoked a stogie, you (cough, cough) have enjoyed two technologies developed by Indians.

We owe those names on the land and a great deal more (the land itself?) to the Indians. I don't think anyone ever bothered to say thanks.

Not Out of the Woods Yet

Have you ever been in a difficult situation when a bit of encouraging news comes, and you said: "... well and good, but we're not out of the woods yet." This odd phrase is an echo from two centuries ago when most of the eastern USA was covered with virgin woodlands. To go cross-country in those far off times was to travel the live-long day in the dim light of the overarching forest. The shade was depressing, even unnerving. You were frequently uncertain as to where you were, how far you had to go still, or whether you had chosen rightly when the track forked three miles back. You had stood there at that fork, puzzling over the blazes on the trees left and right, uncertain as to what they meant.

And as you walked or rode along, you were often worried about what might be lurking behind the next big tree. It could be, and occasionally was, a hungry panther or a rogue black bear. Nothing makes a man's hackles rise more than the thought that something up ahead is waiting to eat him.

Every journey in those pioneer days inevitably ended in a clearing, whether it was a newly sprung-up village or a relative's log cabin. Being "out of the woods" and "in the clear" was always to heave a sigh of relief. Openness and light are cheering to the spirit.

Barking Up the Wrong Tree

P eople who have never fished can have no inkling of the joy of fishing. People who have never hunted can have no idea of the magic of hunting. People who object to hunting and fishing – and they are multitude – have never been really hungry.

Our American ancestors hunted and fished to put food on the table. Necessity drove them to it, but they loved the thrill, and the sense of accomplishment, too. The first man who went hunting at the Jamestown colony in 1607 – probably only a day or two after his ship anchored out in the James River – could hear his own heart pounding and feel his hands shaking when he pointed his blunderbuss at the first browsing deer that wandered past his hiding place. Buck fever! The joy in his heart, and the hope for a juicy venison steak, were wildly dancing when his firearm roared and he saw the animal leap and then go down in a heap. His hand trembled when he drew his knife and walked up to the dying animal to slit its throat and end its misery. He knew that when he returned to the camp with the carcass of the deer draped over his shoulders, he would be greeted by shouts of joy, that he would be admired and counted as a good, useful man. He would eat well, too, he knew, at least until the venison ran out. There are many satisfactions in hunting; body, mind, and spirit.

Two hundred years after that first hunter at Jamestown came striding back into camp with that deer on his shoulders, his descendants were treeing bear and shooting buffalo out in the wilderness six hundred miles further to the west, in Tennessee, Kentucky, and Indiana. Six generations had passed by then, but men still hunted for meat and skins, and for fun, too.

In time, our pioneer forbears discovered that feeding hogs and cattle with their Indian corn multiplied the value of the crop. Over the years their herds grew larger and more numerous. Pork chops and roast beef took the place of bear steaks on the table. As this was happening, during the first decades of the 1800's, wild game gradually grew scarcer. Still, men and boys continued the tradition of hunting, partly to replace their monotonous diet of pork and beef with heartier-flavored squirrel or venison or wild turkey, but mostly for the fun of the hunt.

No animal was more a joy to pursue than a little black-masked cute imp-of-a-critter called "raccoon" today, but invariably referred to as "coon" by the pioneers. It had a fine, heavy pelt, which made for a wonderful winter coat, or a warm cap. Furthermore, a good coonskin might bring a few pennies in trade, too, at the store in the nearby town.

Raccoons were abundant, because they thrived around the farm and the clearing that had sprung up in their original forest haunts. Curious and smart, they quickly discovered the delectable sweet corn patch in the cabin yard. A family of prowling coons could devastate a large garden in a single night. Many a pioneer, on espying the carnage of his sweet corn of an early morning, swore, with narrowing eyes, a blue oath, declaring that Johnny Coon would pay dear, that very night! On other occasions, his wrath against raccoons may have been evoked for other reasons. For example, Mr. Coon invariably discovered the hiding places for the pioneer's hens' eggs, and knew the lip-smacking pleasure of sucking them dry. Many a pioneer wife emitted a yelp of dismay when she discovered, in her secret hen's nest, not eggs, but eggshells! Cute as he was, fastidiously washing his little hands in the creek after savoring his meal, Mr. Coon became the creature the pioneer most enjoyed disliking, though disliking it with real affection.

Our pioneers respected raccoons for a special reason: they were vicious fighters. Woe to the dog that plunged recklessly into the water to attack a retreating coon. He could easily have an ear bitten off, lose a patch of his scalp, or even be drowned if the coon was big enough. Many an old, wise hound learned the hard way not to take on a raccoon in the water, the masked creature's preferred element. When the younger inexperienced dogs of a pack piled snarling into the stream to attack with wild abandon, old Blue would hang back on the shore, content to watch. He had, in modern terms, "been there, done that." He was content to sit back and watch the fun, from a safe distance.

And so the stage was set for the hunting of the raccoon. The best hunting was when the night came down under heavy hanging clouds and still air, for then the scent of Brother Coon would hang like a clinging fog, lingering on the forest path, draped over the rocks of the woodland stream, easy to discover and follow. Two or three experienced dogs were plenty, and always ready. Whining, jumping in happiness, alert in excitement at their night's coming work, they ran happily before the party of two or three hunters striding toward the bluffs above the river bottom. Each hunter carried a lantern in one hand and a rifle in the crook of the opposite arm. They chatted happily but in soft tones, suppressing their excitement. Before long, one of the dogs up ahead would bawl and the spine-tingling sound would echo off the darkened hill, washing over the hunters, who stopped and listened eagerly. A moment later, another of the dogs would join with a higher-pitched call, and finally, older, slower old Blue would join the chorus with his deep, resounding bellow. It raised thrilled hackles on the necks of the hunters, though they had heard it a hundred times already.

In the next minutes the music of the excited dogs receded as they hurried sniffing and running on the trail of the ever-warmer scent of the raccoon, who generally coursed toward the waters of the river. The hunters, listening carefully at the receding cries of the dogs, thrashed through the woods and the brush, getting whipped by branches and stumbling over stumps and roots. Now they would hurry toward the sound of the pack, now pause to listen and adjust their bearing, then rush onward in their new direction while the howls of the hounds echoed magically through the dark, dripping woods.

Aware of the danger now, the raccoon would double on its tracks, leap up and run along a downed tree bole, jump into a streamlet and wade for many yards, all to throw the dogs off its scent. Sometime he would succeed, and the pack would run excitedly back and forth, confused, yelping and whining in disappointment and concern. Sometimes they lost the track altogether, but more commonly they would rediscover it and eventually drive the raccoon up a big tree, somewhere high up on the bluff above the

river. The hunters, hundreds of yards back, would immediately know that the quarry had gone up a tree, for the dogs would bark "treed," a call of a different pitch and sound.

Arriving at the lofty tree where the dogs were leaping and jumping up the trunk, barking and howling in wild excitement, the huffing and puffing hunters would strain their eyes upward for a glimpse of the treed coon, holding up their lanterns in hopes of spotting the glint of the quarry's eyes. The whooping of the dogs, the breathlessness of the hunters' effort, the dark of the night and the thrill of the chase were exciting beyond easy description, intoxicating, like fine whisky.

More than once, the wily raccoon, apprehensive or annoyed at the howling dogs far down below his perch in an ancient beech tree, would tightrope out along an upper branch and leap daringly to the branch of an adjacent tree. There it would scramble to the main trunk and hide in a gnarled branch, or in a hole.

Mr. Raccoon's secret escape happened unbeknownst to the baying dogs, who persisted in trying to clamber up the vertical trunk of the tree first mounted by their quarry. Their frustrated masters, the very nimrods, arriving at last, and not seeing the flash of the eyes of their prey in their lantern lights despite much trying and searching, stood scratching their heads. Eventually they gave a kick in the direction of the dogs, scolded them for their over-eagerness at following a false trail, and gave up and set off in search of a less wily coon.

Thanks to the agility and cleverness of the raccoon, the dogs were barking up the wrong tree.

Corny

Think of the word "corn." Say it out loud. It sounds common and ordinary, doesn't it? Say it again. Isn't there just a faint hint of mystery and meaning in it, too?

Most of us – except those of us who are farmers – have forgotten how important corn is – or, at least, once *was* – though, happily, corn's sun seems to be rising again thanks to the ethanol boom.

To the hardy souls who settled the Midwestern country in the first half of the 19th Century, no single thing – except maybe the rifle – was more important than the sack of corn seed they carried with them. Our pioneers were carrying on a tradition of growing corn first taken up by the Jamestown settlers and by the passengers of the Mayflower. They learned about the crop from the Native Americans and so named it "Indian corn." The term "Indian corn" distinguished it from European term "corn," which in the old country meant "grain," i.e., wheat, oats, or barley.

The Native Americans depended heavily on corn. In the Old Northwest (present day Ohio, Indiana, Illinois, Michigan and Minnesota) Indian cornfields stretched on for miles along the creek bottoms and the river banks near the big Indian towns. European explorers passing into the region were surprised by the size of these plantings and described them in their reports and letters in admiring terms. When the little frontier militia armies from Kentucky penetrated into Indian country north of the Ohio to punish hostile tribes for attacks on their settlements, they always burned the Indians' cornfields and their grain stores. Their winter food supply destroyed, warriors had to hunt to feed their families, and so were prevented, for a season at least, from further attacks on the white settlements.

By whatever name, the tall green plant which poked out big, heavy ears of yellow grain became vitally important for our Midwestern pioneers. They ate corn, in a myriad of forms. They could sell the grain – in the early 1820's it sold for 25 cents a bushel – about $3.25 in today's dollars. And they could feed corn to their livestock, too. The corn stalk became the staff of pioneer life.

With rivers of sweat and back-aching strain the pioneers chopped down the trees and burned them – so they could grow more corn. Virgin timber land – they called it "Congressional land" – purchased for $1.25 an acre from the government could be transformed – through prodigious labor – into corn ground worth $12 an acre. We forget that at the time settlement began, in Indiana, for example, the entire state was one almost unbroken forest. In the northern two-thirds of present-day Indiana, the vast woodlands are now gone, chopped down and burned away – to grow corn. All that is left of the original great woods are patches of woodlots scattered across one vast cornfield (or soybean field – though soybeans are a modern innovation, unknown to our ancestors). Some of the forests in the southern part of the state are gone too, though mostly from the infrequent level areas and the rich river bottoms. Thick hardwood forests still dominate the southern hill country today, mostly because steep hillsides with frequent sandstone or limestone outcroppings are poor places to grow corn. The pioneers had been drawn westward by the dream of rich land. Early reports coming out of Kentucky in the 1770's was the foundation under the dream. On Beargrass Creek, near Louisville, Kentucky, the first farmers reported incredible yields, an unbelievable 30 bushels per acre!

Nearly every man in the early days of the Midwest was a farmer, sometimes in addition to other things he did to earn his bread. The rare exceptions were the storekeepers and public officials like judges and school teachers. Even they sometimes owned farms, and oversaw them on the side. A man's attainments, his standing in society, were judged by the amount of land he owned, and the land he owned was judged by the quantity of corn it could produce.

Corn was pervasive, in the kitchen, the chicken house, the granary and the field. In the early times it had innumerable uses beyond what we normally think about, most of them extremely practical. People slept on corn, for example, at least in the earliest days: Pioneer mattresses were made of corn shucks stuffed into a heavy cloth ticking. These corn pallets were only later replaced by the luxury of featherbeds made from the plumage of chickens or geese – chickens or geese grown fat and feathery thanks to being fed on corn. Little girls played with corn husk dolls, often the only dolls available. A basket of corn cobs in the outhouse was a necessary convenience, one that preceded toilet paper by more than a century. People were tough in those days, and knew from delicate experience what they were talking about when they said that something was "as rough as a cob."

Time was told in reference to the corn crop just as often as to the calendar. Everybody knew when it was roasting ear time, or corn tasseling time. When pioneer friends gathered before the crackling fire on a frosty winter evening the stories often began with the words … "It happened in corn shucking time …" or "It was in corn-planting time …" or "The corn had just been laid by when …" On some of those occasions a jug of liquor was passed around; nearly always it was corn whisky, fermented and distilled from a mash made of at least 80 percent corn grain. It's likely at least one of the listeners smoked a corn cob pipe, having got his start on his noxious habit by smoking corn silks, the always easily-available beginner's substitute for tobacco. If it was an informal gathering, one of those present may have taken off his shoe because his "corns" were hurting – sore spots on the toes due to a pointy deep callus like a corn kernel.

Every farm boy learned to plant corn, and to hoe corn to root out the weeds. He was familiar with the corn rootworm, the corn earworm, the corn leaf aphid that flourished in the dry years, and eventually, the European corn borer. He knew that if the corn had been planted early enough it ought to be "knee high by the Fourth of July" – a standard that our modern corn far exceeds. He knew when it was time to bring in the corn – corn shucking time was in late October and November. After the corn had been harvested he knew how to use a corn knife to slice off the standing stalks so they could be gathered into shocks as fodder for the cattle. And he looked forward to the pleasure of the husking bee, when all the neighbors gathered for a celebration of the harvest. Together they stripped the shucks from the corn, heaping up huge piles of golden ears, while the fiddler played and they danced and told stories late into the night. They knew first-hand what James Whitcomb Riley was talking about when he wrote: "When the frost is on the punkin, and the fodder's in the shock."

Food made from corn was served at virtually every meal. In the evenings, snacks like popcorn and corn parchies provided relief from the boredom, as did popcorn balls fashioned with the help of molasses. In late July and August, sweet corn on the cob, hot and drippy with butter, was a welcome seasonal change of pace. Cornbread, baked in a skillet in the fireplace, was daily fare the year around. It was usually eaten like wheat bread, or taken as cornbread and beans, typical poor man's fare. Variant forms of cornbread included corn pone, corn dodgers, and corn cakes. Corn meal dough fried in hot oil provided delicious corn fritters. Even the meat on the table was mostly based on corn, whether it was corn-fed beef, or fried chicken, boiled eggs or fat-back bacon, because cattle, hogs and chickens were all fattened on corn. Then there was corn pudding and creamed corn, and later canned corn and corn dogs. Corn starch was used in cooking, as was corn syrup. Corn flakes were invented at the end of the 19th century.

Corn – perhaps because it was everywhere and common – gradually became a synonym for bland and dull. When, after the Civil War, baseball became the American pastime, a high pop fly into the outfield that was ridiculously easy to catch came to be referred to as a "can of corn" – nearly beneath contempt for a competent outfielder. In the end, after all that corn and all those years, corn itself became so plain and ordinary as to be almost contemptible. Thus it was that when a man told a joke that was itself plain and bland and whose outcome was utterly predictable, the audience was certain to describe his witticism as nothing more than merely "corny."

On Shooting Oneself in the Foot

I never killed anyone with a gun – to the best of my knowledge, anyway. And even if I did, it wasn't on purpose. Surely I won't be held responsible for a few stray bullets I fired off like a drunken cowboy in a carefree moment. Excuse me, but I was just having fun. If one of those slugs per chance plugged someone – unbeknownst to me, and definitely unintended – I don't think I should be considered at serious fault. It was just a piece of raw bad luck for the bulletary recipient. Yes, I'm sorry it happened (if it did), but what else can I say?

Speaking of luck, I am reminded that in the good old days, when men were men and women wore dresses, there was still such a thing as bad luck. In fact, it was downright common. You saw it every day, out on the street and down the alley. You read about it in the newspaper. People would stop you on the street and tell you the latest instance of it.

Today, things have changed. The bad variety of luck has gone nearly extinct. When something bad happens nowadays everyone jumps up out of their chairs and begins running frantically around looking for someone to blame. In nearly all cases blame is hung like a noose around the neck of a human blame-ee – thanks to the legion of lawyers that infests our society like biting fleas. Today, if a man's dog poops on the sidewalk and the mailman slips on it and cracks his sacroiliac, the dog's owner can be sued, probably *will* be sued. When the same thing happened in the good old days we said that the mailman should have looked where he was stepping, the stupid idiot. The watchword today is "Sue the bastards."

Happily for us old-timers, bad luck still survives, though barely, by the skin of its teeth. For example, not so long ago there was this woman in Georgia who was hit by a meteorite that punched though her roof one night while she was lying in her bed. It bruised the corpulent lady's ample thigh; there was a picture in the newspapers to prove it. A whole convention of lawyers was called in to try to figure out whom to sue. They sensed there was real money to be made! They considered blaming the building contractor because the roof had failed. Trouble was, the house was nearly a hundred years old and the contractor and his business had been dead for half a century. They thought they might somehow implicate the government but they knew that the Town Board had no money, so they gave up on that. They eventually decided that the meteorite's fall was an act of God, and everyone, even lawyers, know that you can't sue God. They finally gave up in despair and repaired to the bar to drink away their frustration. After tipping back a few, elbows on the bar and sad looks on their faces, they finally admitted that the sad event was due to pure bad luck!

OK, OK, back to guns. I grew up in the little coal town of Linton, Indiana, in the mid-1950's. It was a rough-and-tough place, where people shot people from time to time – though only when they felt it was merited. The popularity of firearms and shooting made it easy for me to get acquainted with a big range of manly shooting irons. Just to list the guns (and other missile-related weapons) I've actually fired makes me out of breath: shotguns (10 gauge, 12 gauge, 16 gauge, 20 gauge, 28 gauge, 410 gauge, single-barrel, double-barrel, over-and-under, breech loader, muzzle loader, bolt-action, pump action, semi-automatic); rifles (.22 caliber, 30.06, 30-30, single-shot, pump-action, semi-automatic, lever action); pistols (Colt 45, .38 revolver, German Lugar), bows and arrows (home-made and store-bought); crossbows; pellet rifles (pneumatic, CO2); BB guns; slingshots (which we called bean flippers); bean shooters (a different species from bean flippers); blow pipes; spears (home-made); boomerangs, and miscellaneous rocks and brickbats.

We had *good* luck in the good old days, too. I'll prove it with an example.

Yes, Dammit, the Safety is On

One autumn day my close friend, Rich Luxton – among the brighter flames Linton ever emitted – a witty guy, with a largish head sporting a broad forehead behind which there was impressive gray matter you could see in his large, brown, intelligent eyes – was talked into going hunting with a classmate, a guy by the name of Toploft

Fairlaine. Rich survived, due to good luck, but had reason to regret his decision, as we'll see.

First, picture this Fairlaine guy. He was not without an extra spoonful of brains himself on one side of his brain. He later earned a degree in Civil Engineering at Purdue University (though some people say you don't have to be smart to get an engineering degree, just good at math). Unfortunately, he was a spoon short on the other hemisphere (the empathy and humility side). The real problem was, he was an insufferable smart ass. In the days of Elvis Presley haircuts, Toploft Fairlaine had Elvis fairly beat. His dark brown locks were long, full on the sides and combed into a massive ducktail. The sheaves of glistening hair on top (credit the sheen to Wild-root Cream Oil) could reach down below his nose when he leaned over, but were normally flipped up over his right temple in a big wave that rolled and swirled all the way back to the crown of his cocky head. His little weasel eyes hunched down in the shadows of his pencil-thin eyebrows that rode on beetling brows. From their recesses those deep-set beady eyes steadily scanned you for a weakness that he could belittle and bray over with his scornful staccato laugh. Woe to you if you had a bruise on your cheek, walked with a limp, or had been jilted by your girlfriend. On occasion he pretended to be nice and to be genuinely interested in you and your well-being, but eventually his ruse was outed when you revealed something about yourself that he could ridicule. Then it was har-har-har ad nauseum! He had high cheekbones (suggestive of

Mongol ancestry), between which was planted a nose more like a large unripe strawberry than you will believe. But the central evil in his visage was his thin-lipped mouth, which was always ready to spit out a snarl, a sneer or a wise-crack. Supporting all of the hardware above was the jutting chin of a bully.

Aside from these slight defects, and the fact that he was a coward, there was something charming about him. Part of his magnetism came from his cocksure attitude. When any question was raised or dispute arose, no matter how trivial, he always knew the answer or the explanation, and he was always right, absolutely positively *certain* about it, in short, dead right – until proven wrong. Error he would never admit; instead he concocted some sort of lame explanation before departing the room muttering his flimflammed excuse. One positive trait was that he regularly lost money at our weekly poker games. This endeared him to me, who counted on my $10 or so weekly income from poker as more or less guaranteed when Fairlaine was in the game. Being an easy touch – the kind of guy who would draw to fill an inside straight every time – made him eminently sufferable.

Rich Luxton – whom we have left waiting to go hunting – never thought of himself as a hunter, let alone a Daniel Boone. Thus it was that he was persuaded only with great difficulty to join the rabbit-hunting foray into the bramble-thatched stripper hills north of Linton.

For some reason Fairlaine had decided that Luxton *had* to go, that his presence in the hunting company was absolutely necessary and indispensable. Given the utter necessity of it, he poured all his charm on the adamant Luxton's head; the latter stared into the distance at first, as impervious as a Sherman tank against which mere rocks were thrown, superiorly oblivious of Toploft's pleas. Eventually Fairlaine fell to supplicating and begging, eventually threatening to break into tears if Luxton didn't agree to go along. Fairlaine was capable of beseeching, boot-licking and even sobbing to get his way, and he continued to exert all those talents on Luxton. Embarrassed at last for his friend, Rich finally relented and consented to go.

Stepping out of the car that mid-November day, Fairlaine, Luxton and a third unidentified nimrod shoved shells into their shotguns and set off Indian file along a narrow path that led into rabbit territory. As they strode along, Luxton, who was bringing up the rear, couldn't help but observe that Fairlaine, immediately in front of him, had thrown his gun over his shoulder in typical Elmer Fudd fashion. Its muzzle pointed backwards, directly at Luxton's chest. With mounting alarm, he noticed that Fairlaine's right thumb was hooked in the trigger guard to keep the gun from slipping off his shoulder. Not only that, Fairlaine's thumb was over the trigger. Smart guy that he was, Luxton instantly deduced that a slight stumble or hard jar on Fairlaine's part would likely cause the gun to fall backwards, and that it would be stopped only by Fairlaine's thumb pressing against the trigger. Aware that the path was uneven and that they had to jump over logs and dodge bushes at every other step, Luxton felt distinctly uneasy. The only thing that kept him from a point blank muzzle blast from Fairlaine's blunderbuss was the integrity of the safety lock that prevented the gun from firing. Had Fairlaine remembered to switch on the safety?

"Toploft ...
TOPLOFT!" Luxton called.

Fairlaine stopped, turned slightly, and looked back over his shoulder at Luxton.

"What's wrong?" Fairlaine sneered.

"The way you're carrying that gun makes me nervous. You got your thumb on the trigger. If you stumble it's liable to go off. And guess what? It's pointed right at me most of the time."

Fairlaine sneered. "Ohhhhh Sheeeeee-ittttt, you're an old grandma for sure. There's not a thing to be worried about, you ninny. The safety is on. Watch this ..."

Fairlaine was still holding the shotgun over his shoulder and had his thumb inside the trigger guard. He ostentatiously jerked on the

weapon to mimic a stumble and to demonstrate to Luxton that it couldn't possibly go off.

The reader will guess what happened next. KA-BOOM! The gun roared, sending a blast of pellets into the witch hazel bush beside Luxton, blowing a bushel of brown leaves into the air.

Fairlaine had a look of momentary surprise on his face.

"That's funny," he said, "I thought the safety was on."

Luxton, frozen by the concussion, mouth agape, eyes wide, had a look of horror on his face. He didn't think it was funny. He realized that he had barely escaped ending his life at the age of seventeen, and him still a virgin! Oh God! Had Fairlaine not turned slightly when he gave his demonstration, the muzzle blast of his 12 gauge would have turned Luxton's face into hamburger.

"Where you going?" Fairlaine asked as he watched Luxton hurrying back down the path they had come. After a moment he realized that for some strange reason Luxton had given up hunting for the day.

"What's wrong?" Fairlaine yelled. "Don't you like hunting? It was just a little joke, man! I did it on purpose. There was no harm done, was there? Come on back. All right, you ninny! We're going to go ahead and hunt without you."

They did. Luxton went back to the car and waited there, deciding that he was going to give up the outdoor life permanently and apply himself to more intellectual pursuits. That was fifty years ago. He has never gone hunting since.

Only Use Firearms That Are in Good Working Order

My older brother Jerry was a generous guy, always ready to loan me his stuff. One thing he loaned me nearly got me maimed. For some reason or other I fell into the necessity of borrowing his Ithaca pump-action shotgun at the start of rabbit season one year. It was the 12-guage variety of pump gun, you know, the type where a tube under the barrel is loaded with shells, which are jacked into the firing chamber one-by-one by a quick back-and-forth sliding motion of the hand supporting the front end of the gun. You can shoot a pump gun rapidly, bang! slippety-click, bang! slippety-click, bang!, etc., pulling the trigger immediately when each new shell finds its place in the chamber. The "slippety-click" sound is an awesome one for us gun lovers.

After school one day I went hunting by myself, walking out to Haseman's pasture north of Linton High School. The clumps of briars on the sides of the ditches were good places to kick out cottontail rabbits. The surrounding field was open, and allowed a good shot at the bunny as it bounded away. After climbing over the fence, I loaded five shells into the magazine, and, ducking under the barbed wire, stepped on into the pasture to begin my hunt. A hundred feet in front of me was a thick clump of brambles and grass. As I eyed it, the tingle that all hunters know began creeping up my back. The thought of a rabbit bursting out of the weeds, zigging and zagging towards safety while I drew a bead on him, allowing a proper lead, was already a thrill. And in my mind, at just the right moment I squeeze the trigger and blam! and there before me is the rabbit kicking in its death throes. An unerring shot! Every time! I could see my frontiersmen ancestors smiling down on me.

With this pleasant vision still floating in my mind, I stop while holding the muzzle of Jerry's pump gun pointing at the ground near my right foot. My trigger finger is safely positioned on the outside of the trigger guard. I first check to make sure the safety is switched on so the gun can't fire, then double check. Assured everything is as it should be, I eagerly jack the first shell into the chamber.

Something happens now that I don't instantly comprehend. KA-WHAM! Inches in front of my right foot there opens up a black

hole six inches deep and six inches wide. This is so totally unexpected it takes me several seconds to grasp what has happened: the gun has fired. That isn't possible, I realize. I must have imagined that black hole and the loud bang. Disbelief continuing, I take another step forward, avoiding the black hole in the turf. Yes, it's *impossible* that the weapon has discharged. I'm *sure* the safety was on. I'm *certain* my finger was nowhere near the trigger. I check, double check and triple check. The safety is on "safety." The gun won't fire. I decide that the black hole in the turf is nothing more than a dirty trick by the fates.

Determined to rip myself out of this nightmare and back into reality, I jack a new shell into the magazine. The instant that the motion is complete a second black hole appears by my right foot. In the instant it appears I am rocked by another loud BANG!

Reality now forces me to discard disbelief and acknowledge that every time I throw a new shell into the chamber the gun discharges – even though the safety is on and my finger is nowhere near the trigger.

I gently lay the gun on the ground with trembling hands, all the while staring at the two holes in the ground. If that devil gun had been pointing at my foot when I jacked that shell into the chamber, it would have blown off my foot! Goodbye athletic career!

After fifteen minutes of squatting by that gun, pondering fate and eternity, I finally figured out that the gun wouldn't go off again unless I jacked another shell into the chamber. Relieved at the thought, I gingerly carried the weapon home, pointing it at the sky the whole time, and explained the situation to Jerry. The next day we transported the still hazardous gun to the gunsmith and explained in detail what had happened. After removing the remaining shells, he took the gun apart.

"The sear is broke," he said.

"What's that?" I asked.

"Well, it's a metal part that prevents the gun from firing when a shell is rammed into the chamber."

"Yes, I guess I understand. Thanks a lot."

Thanks a lot to my dad, too, who taught me never to point a gun at a person, or for that matter at anything I wasn't willing to shoot. As I look down at my right foot now, fifty years later, and still count five toes, I reflect the old guy wasn't so dumb after all.

Body Piercing by Smith & Wesson

The only trouble with guns is that they hurt people and make loud noises. If we could do away with the noise and the pain, I believe guns would become far more popular. Even the liberal masses might learn to like them. Thanks to their newfound affection for firearms some of those converts would undoubtedly join the National Rifle Association. Charleton Heston might ascend to Sainthood, thanks to newfound majority support. Anti-gun bumper stickers would disappear. The world would be a better place.

OK, OK, I'm dreaming.

Gun lover that I have always been, I learned early in my shooting career about the pain guns can cause. That's because guns hurt animals and birds, too. In Linton at that day it was quite acceptable to wear a large sheath knife on your belt to school – as long as the blade was less than six inches long. Guns weren't quite that acceptable, but the principal, Mr. Miller, and the teachers weren't much concerned if you kept them out of sight. One of the Meyers (we pronounced their name Mars) boys brought his dad's little revolver to school from time to time. He hid it in his back pocket, as etiquette required. He was a good kid; he honored an unwritten rule by keeping it unloaded, and if asked, would demonstrate that all the chambers were empty by breaking the gun open and spinning the cylinder. He'd also pull some bullets out of his opposite pocket, just to prove that he had some. Another kid (I forget his name) had a little Derringer. It was so small it made no more than a modest bulge in the front pocket of his blue jeans. These little weapons – which would get you one-to-ten years in prison if you carried them to school in today's paranoid climate – were taken for granted then. Yawn. You were far more likely to get hurt when somebody hit you with a snowball with a rock in it and knocked out your eye during a school-sanctioned snowball fight (which happened), or if you fell off the teeter-totters onto your bicycle handle bars and poked the rusty tube into your chest (Billy Joe Baize was his name). There was no lawsuit after Billy Joe's accident, by the way, said injury being judged to be the result of his own stupidity and bad luck.

Like every ten year old kid in those days I had been longing for my own gun since the age of six. I saved my pennies and badgered Mom continually, telling her how pitiful and sad I was not to have a genuine Red Ryder Daisy air rifle, how all of my friends had one already, etc. She told me I could have one as soon as I explained to her why I *needed* one. This was not easy; it took me months to figure that out. I finally broke her resistance when I pointed out that I could keep the blackbirds from eating the grapes in the grape arbor back of the house by shooting them with my BB gun. I guaranteed it. I promised to stand guard nearby, all day long, and shoot any of those dastardly birds that even so much as *looked* at a ripening grape. Eventually she relented, and gave me the two or three additional dollars I needed to purchase my weapon. When she handed over the money, of course, she made me promise not to shoot out the window-lights and not shoot anybody with it, either. I swore I would never do THAT!

I recall it as if it were just an hour ago. There I was, a bright-eyed kid taking the new gun out of the box, oooohing and awwwing, enchanted by the scent of oil and metal, delighted at the big copper BB's that spilled out of the cardboard tube that was part of the package. Its stock was real wood, and there was a leather thong attached to a ring above the lever that served to cock it. It looked all the world like a Winchester Model 70, and I was the proud owner of one. Whoa! Was I somebody, or what?! Was life not good?

Moments later I was wandering around the backyard, looking for something to shoot. I was floating on a cloud of power. I was a man with a gun! I wished that a savage Indian, in war paint, would pop his head up from behind the gooseberry bush. With a BB between his eyes he'd wish he were somewhere else, for sure! None did – word must have gotten around that I had a gun now. There was not even a blackbird or an English sparrow to be seen. The neighborhood cats were keeping out of sight, too – they must also have heard about me and my gun.

For a time I amused myself by shooting at tin cans I set up in the alley. This soon became boring. Noticing the big silver city water tower that loomed a hundred yards to the east of the alley, I selected that as my next target. It was 125 feet high, topped by a giant silver water tank on which "LINTON" was painted in two-foot high black letters. Aiming at the top, pffffttt went the air rifle. This was followed – after a delay of two or three seconds – by a faint ping. What a delightful sound! After a few dozen such shots, I became bored with this, too.

An evil spirit gradually crept into my brain, whispering "kill something, kill something, you've got to KILL something." Evil, the urge to kill, took over me; I became unreasoning, driven by the need to take something's life.

I was sitting under the grape arbor as this thought plunged its fangs into me, my Daisy lying across my lap. Just then an orange-breasted robin – the most harmless of birds – hopped into view. It was hunting for earthworms, stopping every few feet and cocking its head to the side to listen. From time to time it would peck and draw back its head with a wriggling fishing worm writhing in its beak. Robins aren't much afraid of people but are always careful not to let you come closer than a few feet from them. This was a young one, its orange breast just coming into its full color.

I slowly raised my Red Ryder Daisy Air Rifle and ... I'm sad to confess it ... broke its neck with my first shot. It flopped around for several seconds, emitting a pitiful peeping. As I stood over it, its glistening eyes watched me like I was the hovering angel of death, an undeserved death, for that poor creature. Moved by the awful thing I had done, I could stand the mournful peeping no longer. I raised my gun again and put a BB through its head, ending its misery.

My misery had just begun. It dawned on me that I had killed a harmless creature. I picked up the poor bundle of feathers that had been a living thing moments before, and took it and buried it in the garden, muttering a prayer, begging forgiveness for my cruelty.

When I passed though the kitchen on the way to my room, Mom asked,

"What's wrong?"

"Nothing," I said.

I didn't shoot that BB gun for days after that. I had learned remorse.

Random Acts of Violence

I eventually recovered from my regrets over killing that harmless robin and continued my career as a hunter and shooter. A year or two later some buddies and I started a game we called BB gun war. We went out to the stripper hills north of town and divided ourselves into two equal-sized gangs. The object was to shoot the opponent soldiers before they shot you. If you were hit by a BB, you were out, and were required to sit down under a tree until there was just one last man standing. One of the rules was that you couldn't shoot anyone in the head. My career as a BB soldier ended one day when, sneaking up on one of the enemy, I raised my head over a log, trying to figure out just exactly where the guy was. I took a BB in the face. It made a big red dot, exactly one inch below my left eye, and it stung like a wasp. I had to make up an excuse for Mom when I got home. She would have been horrified if she knew it was a BB wound. I lied – for her sake – and to keep from getting an endless lecture on my stupidity. I was fully aware of my stupidity and didn't need to be told. I never played that idiotic game again.

There were other incidents that I recall with shame, or horror. In high school I ran with a couple of guys who were as rebellious as I, Dick Haseman and Jerry Brown. We'd take our rifles and go camping. One night, after sharing a pint of cherry vodka at our campsite in the Greene-

Sullivan State Forest, we fell asleep. In the middle of the night Haseman thought he heard something. Bigfoot was out there in the darkness, he thought. He shook us awake and we piled out of the tent, rifles at the ready. The campfire had died down to a few embers and the silence was ominous. Suddenly a twig snapped in the distance. We snapped too, and commenced firing our .22 semi-automatics wildly in all directions. The night was turned into orange streaks of fireworks from our muzzle blasts. We probably shot off 200 rounds, stopping only when we were out of ammunition.

The next morning a game warden appeared. He asked if we had been shooting off our guns last night. He said that some people camping across the lake heard bullets whizzing through the trees above their tent, and had complained. We admitted that we had heard some shooting, but it wasn't us, no sir! The officer knew we were lying, but what could he do? He had made his point. He told us not to come back there any more.

The same two friends of mine, who were nice fellows (Haseman later became an Indiana State Trooper), helped perpetrate another act of mayhem. It developed in the same senseless way as the campground shoot-out. We were wandering through a distant woods north of Linton one day, our .22 rifles at our shoulders. Haseman spotted something moving in a tree high above. He raised his rifle and started firing away at the things that were moving up there. It seemed that treetop was crawling with animals. Brown and I started firing, too. Moments later furry things started dropping around us like it was raining cats and dogs. But it was raccoons instead: the mother coon, whose entrails were hanging out thanks to a hollow-point bullet tearing through her gut, came down first, then her seven babies. When the shooting was over and the mother and her seven children (cute beyond words) were put out of their misery with shots to the head, I was sick at heart at the terrible senseless thing we had done, and determined never to do anything like that ever again. I didn't, not even close. It was another dose of remorse like with the innocent robin, but far bigger.

Quick-Draw McGraw

Western movies and TV shows thrilled us in the '50's and early '60's. High Noon with Gary Cooper held us spellbound in 1952. We admired Alan Ladd as a courageous sheepherder in cattle country in Shane (1953). John Ford's The Searchers featured that real man, John Wayne (1956), while the Gunfight at the O.K. Corral (1957) starred Kirk Douglas and Burt Lancaster. The Magnificent Seven was a grand box office hit in 1960. At the same time, TV was competitive, offering us "Gunsmoke" beginning in 1955 and Bonanza in 1959.

We loved those shows because the men portrayed were courageous, willing to stand up for their rights against long odds and use their six-guns to fight for what they believed. Rather than getting a lawyer and going to court to redress their grievance against a bully —

they shot the bastard. It was simpler that way. You left the movie house feeling satisfied.

With all that gunplay and with so many Wyatt Earps, Doc Holidays and Wild Bill Hickocks setting an example for young and old, it's no wonder that shooting irons became popular with us. Everybody who considered himself a real man (even though he was still a boy) had to have a six-shooter. The best of them got a hip holster as well, and sought to become adept at quick-draw shooting. The popularity of this pastime faded fast, though, because the he-men who aspired to expertise in the art insisted on using live ammunition. Would real men use blanks? Hardly! There followed such an epidemic of self-inflicted wounds that the hospital emergency rooms had to put on extra staff. The commonest wounds included bullets in the thigh, self-kneecapping (well before the Italian mobsters thought of it), and foot-shooting. Now and then a rare unfortunate who had insisted in keeping his six-shooter thrust down the front of his pants, turned up with a more serious wound – delicacy prevents me from describing it here. Eventually it dawned on the survivors that they should follow four rules: (1) don't use hollow-point bullets – they make really ragged wounds; (2) don't pull the trigger until the gun is out of the holster (or your waistband); (3) don't aim the gun at any part of your own

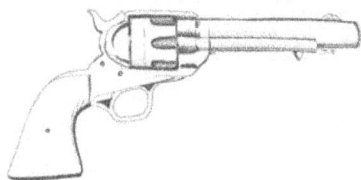

anatomy while pulling the trigger; and (4) take up bowling or croquet, they are far safer and pose no threat to your anatomy.

Three Cheers for Guns

Where would we be without guns, after all? The Indians would have driven the colonists back into the sea, wouldn't they? And our ancestors would have starved to death because they had no guns for hunting food – and where would that have left us? – quite obviously, only wimpy vegetarians would have survived. Guns have been such a part of our lives that words and phrases referring to firearms and shooting have penetrated deeply into our English language.

Which of us hasn't been called a "son of a gun," a fairly gentle reference to the legitimacy of our birth and a hint that our mother's morals were, say, *questionable.* No wonder that if something has been a threat to us once, and we learned to fear it, we became gun shy at the prospect of confronting it again. If we want to show off our car, we may gun the engine to impress someone with its power. When we are under threat if we don't complete a task on time, we are under the gun. Of course it may be a long shot that we will complete the task on time. Everyone goes off half cocked from time to time, don't they? And bright prospects that quickly dim are no more than a flash in the pan.

This essay is over now; if I go on any longer I'm afraid I may shoot myself in the foot.

A Lot of Bull!

If you've ever stood next to a living, breathing full-grown dairy bull, it's safe to say that you were impressed. Let's suppose you tip the scales at a beefy 220 pounds – don't worry ladies, I'm not talking about you – and so you justifiably consider yourself a hefty hunk. Well, when you place yourself beside a hearty Holstein bull that weighs two thousand you can't avoid noticing that you are by comparison a mere puny pipsqueak. The offensive line of the Indianapolis Colts doesn't weigh as much as that bull. Yes! It *is* a brute!

Don't get too close to him. There's a reason he has a ring in his nose.

The reason for the ring is that any run-of-the-mill bull is big enough to go anywhere he wants to go and do anything he wants to do when he wants to do it – if he isn't restrained somehow. A strong fence may hold him under ordinary circumstances, but if he really gets his juices flowing and decides he wants to be on the other side because, well, maybe, a cow on the other side is throwing flirting glances his way, he'll walk right through it.

Such prodigious animal power has excited awe from man and boy, young and old, down the centuries. The stockman of yore, owner of such power, had to find a way to control it before he could truly possess it.

Hidden somewhere behind the obscuring mists of history an ancient herdsman probably first stumbled upon the key trick. He discovered – likely thanks to a mixture of bad and good luck – that the bull, giant though he is, has an Achilles heel – located on the opposite end of his body – his nose.

How this discovery was made is easy to imagine. In a careless moment, having inadvertently provoked his bull, the suddenly maddened animal knocks down the hapless herdsman and proceeds to use its huge head to pound him into the ground. With no prospect of getting up again and running away, the poor fellow does the only thing left to him: he sticks his thumb and fingers into the bull's nostrils and pinches for dear life – literally!

The effect on the bull is nothing less than miraculous: in the instant the fingers enter his nose he goes from raging to disengaging (or at least desiring to disengage), ceases his attack and becomes as docile as a lamb. The herdsman then struggles to his feet – still holding the bull's nose in his fingers – and leads it to its stall in the barn where he can safely let go.

In time, the custom arose of inserting metal nose rings into the nostrils of young bulls. The ring was punched through the grisly nasal septum and thereby fixed firmly and permanently in place. It provided a convenient handle to grab in case of an emergency. More commonly – to prevent such emergencies from occurring in the first place – a halter or lead chain was passed through the ring. Thanks to halter and nose ring the biggest bull could be led around like the most docile of old dogs.

An alternative to nose rings were bulldogs. Stockmen, who in days of yore valued dogs for the useful services they performed, had long known that a good dog, properly trained, could subdue an unruly bull. This involved the dog grabbing the bull's nose in its powerful jaws and hanging on for dear life – until the bull, paralyzed by the agony, gave up the fight and stood submissively, head bowed, with the dog still hanging on its snout.

The discovery that dogs can subdue bulls and live to tell about it (via the scars they bore, of course, as well as by their masters' bragging in the pub) gradually led to a public entertainment that pitted a brave dog against a tethered bull.

This was called bull-baiting. This sport was at first a mere rustic village entertainment attended by a few farmers and local yokels, but as the years passed and word of the excitement of David (dog) taking on Goliath (bull) spread far and wide, gentlemen and even people of the noble classes showed up to watch the fun and place bets on the outcome.

It was indeed an extraordinary spectacle to see a determined little dog take on an immense bull and rag it into submission – forcing the bovine to cease attacking or even struggling – thanks to the dog clinging tightly, its iron jaws clamped in the tender flesh of the bull's snoot. The pluck and pertinacity of particularly outstanding bulldogs came to be renowned across the countryside. During these exciting contests the dogs danced and dodged around the bull, waiting for a chance to grab its ear or its nose, while the bull roared, snorted and swung its mighty head at the annoying little creature below it. Dogs that moved too slow were sometimes flung over the heads of the spectators by a toss of the bulls head. Remarkably, they always returned to the attack despite being bloodied, gored or even having broken bones – their pertinacity always excited the wonder and admiration of the crowd. The story is told of the incredible spirit of one dog that had its entrails ripped out by the bull's horns, yet returned gamely to the attack while the crowd cheered wildly. We, of course, condemn such a "blood sport" as something terrible and brutal.

The pinnacle of bull-baiting was reached about two centuries ago. It took the form of the English bulldog. This particular manifestation of the canine was built low to the ground making it harder for the bull to reach it with its horns or its pile-driving head. The bulldog's face was covered with flaps of wrinkled skin, which allowed the blood it drew to drain away from the high-set eyes. Its nose was flat, which allowed its under-set jaw to get a more powerful grip on the bull's tender snout. The bulldog's head was massive and its shoulders and front legs were heavily muscled. This weight distribution brought the center of gravity forward, making it harder for the bull to fling off. Aficionados of bull-baiting justified their sport by the doubtful claim that a good struggle between bull and dog caused the bull's otherwise tough old flesh to become more tender and flavorful. Despite its popularity, in 1835, bull-baiting was outlawed in England.

Not surprisingly, the bulldog soon fell out of favor among breeders. Even so, it still survives as a breed today, ugly as ever, yet loving and gentle, the viciousness long since bred out of it. It's nice to know that no matter how ugly you are, someone will love you – especially if you have a sweet disposition.

A different form of bull fighting still survives, in Spain and in parts of Latin America. Opinions of the sport are passionate and polarized, but modern bull-fighting differs from bull-baiting in one particular – it pits a *human* against a bull. The bull has a chance (albeit small) to survive and occasionally tramples and gores the bull fighter to death, tossing him around like a limp rag. In truth, it's a fairer contest, but a more interesting one because it involves a man or sometimes even a woman (one of the questionable triumphs of women's liberation).

The spectacle of modern bull-fighting touches something deep in the human spirit, with the bull representing brute nature, as did the minotaur of ancient times, while the matador represents man, namely Theseus, who killed the minotaur and so arrived at full manhood. The awe of the modern contest between man and bull – a struggle of skill, art, and beauty where a young man with a red cape and a sword faces a pawing, angry bull whose horns can kill, while thousands watch and cheer, was told compellingly by Ernest Hemingway in his "Death in the Afternoon." Our literature has been enriched by other books about bullfighting. The reader who has never opened the pages of "Or I'll Dress You in Mourning" by Larry Collins and Domenique Lapierre – the story of a Spanish peasant who triumphed over crushing odds to become the most famous of all Toreadors, "El Cordobes" – has missed one of the great stories of the human spirit.

We Americans invented our own bull ritual: bull riding. It's thrilling to watch, knowing that the brave (insane?) cowboy on the back of that giant Brahma bull is nearly certain to get flung off. If he persists at this sport for long, it is inevitable that he will be gored, trampled or flung into unconsciousness by the plunging, whirling brute on whose back he attempts to stay for a mere eight seconds. Jim

Shoulders, one-time World Champion Cowboy, had dozens of broken bones in his career, many of them thanks to being thrown by bulls. To these injuries were added countless lesser ones, like dislocated joints, ripped ligaments and torn muscles. Bull riders and the bulldogs of old have a lot in common – pluck!

The old Greek Aesop, that bubbling fountain of folk wisdom, knew how imposing bulls are, and passed on to us several fables involving them. His respect is evident in his story of a gnat that settled on the horn of a bull, and sat there a long time. Just as the gnat was about to fly away, he made a buzzing noise, and asked the bull if he would like him to go. The bull answered, "I did not know you had come, and I shall not miss you when you are gone." The moral of Aesop's story is that some men (or women) are of more consequence in their own eyes than in the eyes of their neighbors.

Bulls so impressed our ancestors that words and phrases related to them still color our everyday speech, sometimes in funny ways. Everyone has participated in bull sessions, even delicate women. What were those people doing, anyway? - Just shooting the bull. And it's amusing to reflect, for example, that many a determined man who has never in his life laid eyes on a living bull will nevertheless boldly confront a hazardous or unpleasant task (whether physical or otherwise) while declaring that he is going to take the bull by the horns. If you try to talk him out of it, he'll likely refuse, bullheaded cuss that he is. In attempting to dissuade him we have his best interest at heart, of course; we just want to be sure that he doesn't wade into a fragile situation like a bull in a china shop. If needed, we may call for assistance from his girlfriend, who, everyone knows, leads him around by the nose (or like he has a ring in his nose). We have to be careful not to provoke the guy, for the smallest insult is like waving a red flag in front of a bull.

The word "bull" is sometimes used for rather small things that are merely relatively large, like bullfinches, bull thistles, and bull frogs. But mostly "bull" has come to represent big and powerful; think of a bulldozer shoving down trees and pushing around huge piles of earth. Nothing is more imposing than a bull moose – back before World War I Teddy Roosevelt named his splinter political party after that imposing brute. American history has been marked by bulls in other ways – most of us have heard of the Battle of Bull Run (actually there were two of them) – but few people have the slightest notion what a bull run is. I assume they consider Bull Run to be the name of a little waterway. Wrong!

Bulls can be symbols of good, too. Wall Streeters strongly prefer a bull market over the bear market. In the hope that you will invest your money with them, the brokerage house of Merrill Lynch proudly declares that it is bullish on America. A target shooter – whether he is shooting arrows, throwing darts,

or firing an elephant gun – always aims for the bullseye. Bull Durham tobacco was sold in little white cloth pouches and was enormously popular in the days when men rolled their own cigarettes. That product faded away and was displaced by a much more convenient one called Marlboro. A popular energy drink of today – a powerful concoction of sugar and caffeine – is marketed under the name of Red Bull.

I'm going to end this essay before you declare that it is nothing more than a cock and bull story.

You'll have to admit that it *is* a lot of bull.

Stump Speech

Nothing is more American than the stump speech. Today, in election season, we still hear the term. In pioneer days, as today, politicians needed an audience and it was not easy to find one. The campaigner could hardly go from door to door, since doors were sometimes a mile or more apart. Churches were rare, too, or not yet existent, and so he couldn't meet people there either. There was a special problem with churches, anyway: if the candidate was a Methodist he could hardly go to a Baptist or a Quaker or a Catholic meeting. We moderns have to remember that people took religion *seriously* in those days. A Baptist at a Methodist meeting would have been glowered at by the congregation and pitied as a lost soul on his way to Hell. No right-thinking Methodist would vote for *him*! No, religious gatherings were poor places to campaign. The tolerant ecumenical spirit was far in the future.

Would-be audiences were indeed hard to find. There was of course no radio, no TV and no internet. Newspapers might come to mind as a way to reach people, but they were printed in distant cities, expensive, almost always out of date, biased, and the settler might wait a month or two between issues.

So how did the office-seeker get the ear of the voters? For scores of years, roughly the first half of the 19th century – from 1815

to 1875 in current Indiana – the settlers grappled with the colossal task of clearing the forests. In the beginning the trees were literally everywhere, except in the scattered prairies or in the river bottoms. When the white man first came into the region that eventually became Indiana, fully 90 percent of the land was covered in forest. The pioneer's road to prosperity involved turning low-value woodland into high-value farmland. He did this by means of a sharp axe and a strong back. An enterprising man with a few strapping sons could turn government land bought at $1.25 an acre into prime farm ground worth $12.00 or more an acre, merely by cutting down the trees.

Merely! It was an enormous labor, almost beyond imagining for us today. When a man brought his family and purchased land from the government, the first thing he did was girdle trees on the part of

his land he thought would make the best crop ground. Girdling involved chopping a two-inch wide trough through the bark completely around the circumference of the tree. When spring came, the tree, its circulatory system cut, failed to leaf out. The pioneer then planted his first crop among the still-standing dead trunks. The area was called the "deadening," actually, in Indiana, the settlers described it as the "dednin." In the subsequent autumn, after the crop had been harvested, or in the following early spring, he started felling the dead trees, and chopping out their tops. His future cornfield was soon littered with scores of large logs. His problem then was how to get rid of the corpses of all those forest behemoths. The answer was: cut them up and burn them. But this was far too much work for one man to do. It would take him years to do it without help. This is where his friends and neighbors came in. Word was passed around for miles in every direction that help was needed on a certain date. There would be a log-rolling!

Men, women and children came, commonly scores of them, arriving on foot, in their wagon, or on horseback, always followed by their dogs, who enjoyed social events too, and wouldn't be left at home for anything. Everybody worked hard, chopping, rolling, and burning the logs the-live long day, but there was joy in it, too.

Men who prided themselves on their skill with the axe – and most men figured they were as good as any with that implement – seized every opportunity to demonstrate how rapidly they could chop through a three foot trunk. Happy to be noticed, they made the chips fly. Young men were particularly eager to prove their strength and energy. They bustled from log to log, hacking away, hopeful of catching the eyes of the pretty young women, prospective brides who brought jugs of water and smiles. Some of them were truly beautiful, at least in the young bachelors' eyes.

All the women, young and old, busied themselves with the meal, making corn bread, sweet potatoes, boiled potatoes and dandelion salad. They fried venison and beef and chicken, sizzling it in lard in big black iron skillets. Each of them, young and old, had brought from home a crock full of their favorite recipe, hopeful of a compliment. Maybe it was baked beans and bacon made with maple sugar, or deviled eggs, or a sweet cherry pie. The girls of marriageable age were especially eager to hear a word of praise from a young man who had caught their eye, the one they thought most handsome and strong, and gentle, too, a perfect prospective husband.

The older children busied themselves "niggering off" logs (my apologies to political correctness, but this is what they called the process), that is, burning through them by a peculiarly effective technique: a groove was cut in the top of the log, and a fire started in the groove using dry wood chips and tinder. Once that fire was burning well, they laid a green pole from a fresh-cut sapling in the groove and heaped more chips and tinder over it. By keeping weight on the sapling-pole, and feeding the fire with fresh dry chips, the sapling burned through the log with surprising speed, like a burning knife. One long log thus became two shorter ones, quickly enough, with both severed ends blackened and charred.

The younger children chased one another, played tag and catch and hide-and-seek. The dogs romped after one another, barking in excitement and sniffing one another's rumps. They rambled and snuffled around among the choppers and the burners, pausing only to shake an unfortunate snake to death in their jaws, or to dispatch a surprised skunk. All in all, it was exciting beyond description, with the thock-thocking of the wood choppers, the yells of "heave" or "timber" by the woodsmen, with the scent of burning wood mixed up with the aroma of cooking food in their noses, all this amidst the sounds of barking dogs and the excited laughter of children. It was a community like we in the twenty-first century can hardly imagine, and it is gone forever.

After some hours of this joyful, sweating toil, with the tree trunks all cut into manageable sections, the men gathered together in teams, each with his pry pole. They rolled the logs into piles by brute strength, aided only by adept application of the principles of physics. Sometimes they heaped the logs around any still-standing deadened trees, or piled them around the larger stumps.

Stumps were a particular concern to the land owner because he knew that when he plowed behind his horse next spring, he faced the real danger that his plowshare would hook on a big root hidden near a stump, whereupon the plow (and himself) might be flung violently to the ground. Ridding the land of stumps and big roots was the hardest task of all, so hard that when a man confronted a particularly difficult problem, one almost insolvable at the first attempt, he would declare that he was "stumped."

Jugs of whisky were always available to lighten the labor, and for refreshment and encouragement. But generally the men were allowed to drink only as a reward, as when a particularly big log had been rolled to its place on the pile.

When all was finally ready, commonly in the later part of the afternoon, the fires were set. Within minutes, a dozen huge pyres scattered over several acres sent the bodies and souls of the once-giants of the forest into the sky in a cloud of gray smoke, with a thunderous crackle and roar.

Later on, while the pyres popped and roared on the cleared acres roundabout, the pioneer dinner was spread on plank tables set up for the purpose. Everybody was famished from their work, or play, but they couldn't eat just yet. First they had to hear a loud, and often windy, blessing by the most distinguished preacher in attendance. Like everyone else, he relished the opportunity to be seen and heard, especially the chance to demonstrate his piety and way with words. Only after the loud chorus of Amens echoed down the hollow did the tired but happy pioneers finally eat. Stuffing themselves with gusto while the womenfolk hurried and hovered around, solicitous that their plates not get emptied, they talked and joked and enjoyed the satisfaction of good work done and a powerful appetite stilled.

Now, at last, the men who were ambitious for public office had their chance. They had worked hard and long, too, because they knew they had to be respected to be elected, and a man who couldn't chop with the best of them and heave and strain with vigor, while cracking jokes with good-natured cleverness, was not respected. A man with the reputation for being lazy had no chance at all.

The politician's platform was often a three-foot high stump at the edge of the gathering. Up there he would leap, as the shadows of evening lengthened, and with waving arms, looking all the voters boldly in the eye, he would hold forth in a loud confident voice. He didn't neglect to extol his high principles and singular virtues, with a touch of modesty, of course. He was careful not to use too many big words, for he had at all costs to avoid being considered "uppity." And he never forgot to praise his party, too, whether it be Whig or Democrat. If he was an especially good talker, and well-liked, and could turn back a heckler's smart crack with a good-natured retort of his own and so get the crowd to laugh, he was thought to be clever and a good man and his hopes of election were much enhanced.

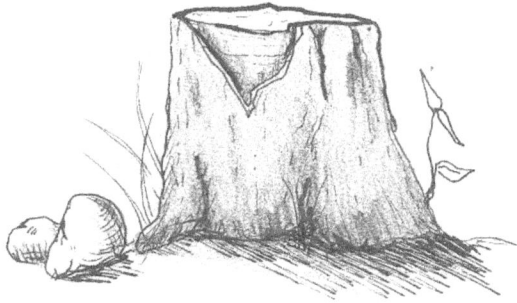

So it was that meeting and impressing the voters came to be known as stumping. It was in this pioneer setting that stump speeches took their origin, and men learned to let the chips fall where they may, and try never to be stumped.

Hold Your Horses!

e hardly ever have occasion to remember that the noble steed (or the sway-back mare) was once the standard means of transportation. A century after the automobile began carrying us from town to town at breathtaking speed, we are still, from time to time, told to "hold our horses." This is a throwback to the days when a nervous, neighing and prancing team of equines occasionally threatened to bolt and wildly drag a wagon-load of frightened passengers down the road lickety-split into the jaws of disaster. The fault usually lay with the driver, who didn't exert firm control over his excitable brutes. Instead, they controlled him, and impatiently trotted off, or even ran away, before it was time.

These days we hardly ever think about the benefits of the transition from horse-under-the-saddle to horsepower-under-the-hood. Think, for example, about the absence of piles of horse apples in the road, and the disappearance of the heavy smell (some would call it a stink) of the town livery stable. The banishment of the horse from our neighborhood streets caused much more to vanish as well: the hitching post, the town saddle maker, the feed bag, the ringing hammer of the neighborhood blacksmith, and even the clatter of the horse cavalry. These days, when the horse has been gone from our streets for nearly a century already, we can't help wondering about the eventual fate of the horse laugh, the horse face, and horsing around. It's true that we do still occasionally meet someone who smells like a horse, or hear of someone beating a dead horse. We know that powerful cars will always have a lot of horsepower, even though the guy behind the wheel may not have much horse sense.

There is still more to the good side of the decline of the equine. Horse flies have become rare and we should be grateful, for they packed a walloping bite. And we no longer hear of people missing work because they were kicked by a horse, thrown by a horse, bitten by a horse, or horsewhipped by a villain. Ah! The good old days!

Going to the Mill

More than half a century ago, when I was a wee tot and needed to be diverted from mischief, my mother played a game with me which she herself had played when she was little. She called it "Going to the Mill." It was a simple game. All it took to play was a piece of chalk and a writing slate. On a frosty winter's day, while the older kids were at school, we would sit on the floor by the glowing pot-bellied coal stove in the living room, the slate beside us. I would take the chalk in one hand, put both my hands behind me out of sight, and then pass the chalk back and forth between my hands until inspiration whispered to me which one to hide it in. I then made fists of both hands – with the

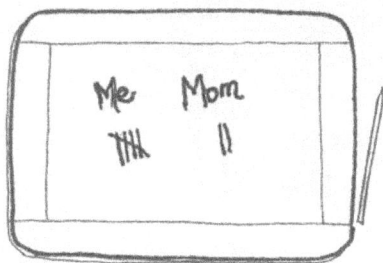

chalk hidden in one of them – and presented both outstretched hands to Mother. She had to guess which of my little hands concealed the chalk. If she guessed wrong, I earned a point, which was duly recorded as a chalk mark on the slate. I also won the privilege of hiding the chalk again. If Mother guessed the proper hand, then I gave the chalk to her so she could hide it. If she succeeded in fooling me, she got to make a mark on her side of the slate. Thus the chalk passed back and forth in a fun guessing game – fun at least for the five-year old that was me. The winner was the first one to get 10 marks on the slate.

If you are thinking that this was a primitive game, you're right. Cave men could have played it, it's that simple. But it was not without value. Besides passing the time and keeping me out of trouble, it helped me learn useful things. To count, for example. And it taught me that you can use chalk marks to represent numbers. It also provided a lesson (unconsciously, of course) that reaching a distant goal requires many steps, and that the journey is sometimes plagued with delays and bad luck – in this case a run of good guesses on the part of my opponent. The game stimulated my imagination, too: In my foggy child's consciousness, I happily imagined that each mark on my slate represented one actual step closer to the mill, each a matter for excitement and pride. It also taught me psychology and reverse psychology. I soon figured out that if I randomly distributed the chalk in my left or my right hand, and my opponent herself guessed randomly, that it was a matter of mere luck as to who got to the mill first. However, if I applied certain devious tricks – such as holding one hand (the one empty of the chalk) slightly forward of the other, it increased the odds that my opponent would pick that one. I also learned that feigning a sad face at the right moment – just as Mother's hand hovered indecisively over my empty hand – was sometimes enough to convince her to choose that hand. What fun to fool people with a trick! The game taught me to believe that I was clever, too, though I now know that my mother was always a knowing sucker for my tricks. She let me win almost every time – out of her generous loving spirit – except when she was exasperated with me and felt that I needed to be taken down a notch or two.

I've often wondered who taught Mother that game, and where it got its name. I think it was her grandfather, Asa Burdsall, who taught her. He was a Civil War veteran and retired farmer who spent a lot of time with Mother during her girlhood in the years before and just after the First World War. Asa grew up in the hill-surrounded valley of the Muscatatuck River, in Jackson County, Indiana, a few miles south of Brownstown. He was born there in 1841, one of a large family, on a primitive farm. In those days, as elsewhere in pioneer Indiana, wheat and corn had to be ground into flour. Corn meal or wheat flour that had been stored too long got bugs in it, or musty and moldy, or went stale and had to be replaced. Or else the supply was just used up. And so it was that from time to time someone had to carry the grist to the mill.

It was a big day in every pioneer boy's life when his mother called to him for the very first time – this must have happened to Asa – and said: "Son, saddle the mare and take this sack of wheat to the water mill to be ground! Your pa wants some fresh wheat bread when he comes home from the field this evenin'." With what swelling pride and dignity did the boy assume this manly duty?! Riding the mare all by himself! And a whole three miles over to Mill Creek to boot, where the Staley brothers kept a big imposing water-driven mill!

A high responsibility indeed, it was! No doubt the boy sat tall in the saddle, particularly when he trotted haughtily past his erstwhile playmates at the neighboring cabin down the valley. There they stood, stopped in their play, mouths agape, staring in astonishment and grievous envy. "Look at him! He's riding the mare! He's going to the mill!" Asa may have pretended not to notice them, insignificant as they were. Oh! He was a proud one, near to manhood now, rambling off as he did through the countryside, as imperious as a knight-errant on a noble charger, on a mission vital to the well-being of his family.

Water-driven grist mills were a central part of pioneer life in Indiana. Everyone, man, woman, and child, was familiar with their giant course-grained white limestone wheels. Driven by the great wooden water wheel attached to the stones by a small miracle of engineering, they ground the grain fine, white and pure.

The ideas and images of the neighborhood grist mill came to be woven through the fabric of pioneer lives, and were reflected in their thoughts and speech. And so the average man or boy facing a heavy problem imagined that he had a "millstone around his neck," an undesirable state indeed. Or when these pioneer folks confronted the prospect of returning to a dull, repetitive task, it was "back to the old grind." If groups of them were wandering aimlessly in circles, they were "milling around," going nowhere, like a millstone. When a man was presented with an abundance of materials on which to work, it was "grist for his mill." If a woman was exhausted and worn down with her labors, she had been "through the mill."

Those old water wheels, with their massive grinding stones, rhythmically clicking, groaning and thumping above the music of rushing water, are gone forever now, washed away by some long-forgotten spring flood a century ago. If they come to our minds at all, it is only when we imagine the tranquility of the old mill pond, or maybe think nostalgic thoughts of a leisure hour spent down by the old mill stream. Hoagy Carmichael, quintessential Hoosier, born in 1899, was just the right age to grasp the meaning of this part of the slowly vanishing past. His 1931 song, which began with the words "Up the lazy river," became immensely popular, had, for its second line: "By the old mill run."

Backlog

I realize that your toothache is painful, Mr. Murdock," my dentist tells me over the phone, "but I have a large backlog of patients. I'm sure we can squeeze you in, in just three weeks. Sorry, but I have an early flight for Bermuda tomorrow morning. Call my nurse tomorrow and she will be happy to set up an appointment. Goodnight."

"But, BUT ..!!" I sputter through my tooth-aching clenched jaw as I hear the hang-up click.

Regrettably, our hectic twenty-first century lives are jammed with backlogs. At the cleaners, at the bookstore, at the car mechanic, at the computer store, in the government, at work, morning, noon, and midnight. Backlogs! We hate them.

It's enough to make us pine for a simpler time, for pioneer days, when there were real backlogs. In those long gone days, people loved backlogs. Then, the hearth and fireplace were the heart and soul of every pioneer home, no matter how poor the family. Here was refuge from the labors of the day, here the place where the man of the house, in from chopping trees the live-long day in the chill of frosty January, could pull off his boots and warm his numb feet at the roaring fire. Here the woman of the

house would bustle at boiling stew and baking cornbread in her Dutch oven to feed her famished flock. Here, in the evenings, she would spin flax or cotton, and listen to the click of her wheel in rhythm with the flickering fire. Here the children would assemble of an evening, parching corn and telling their adventures of the day. Hearth and home came to mean the same thing.

The true heart of a home in the American woods of the early 19th century, though, was the fire itself. It was necessary for light in the mostly windowless cabins, essential for warmth, and indispensable for cooking. No wonder people, upon leaving for a journey, used to say to one another – an admonition tinged with sadness – "Keep the home fires burning."

There was good reason for that. To let the fire in the fireplace go out was to let darkness into the house, and hunger, too, and even cold. A dead fire in the summer was bad. In the winter it was nigh onto an emergency. Something had to be done about it quick. There were no matches in the house, certainly no pilot lights or cigarette lighters, no thermostat to turn up, only flint and steel. Using these primitive implements to start a fire was tedious, difficult, and uncertain. Commonly the fireless family would send one

of the older children running through the woods to the nearest neighbor's cabin, sometimes a mile or more away, carrying a covered metal fire-pan in hand. The child would fetch glowing coals from the neighbor's fire and hurry back home. Here the coals would be used, together with some tinder, to get a good blaze licking again.

It was better yet not to let the fire go out at all. The problem was how to prevent that from happening.

The secret was the backlog, literally the back log in the fireplace. After the cold fireplace was cleaned out, the backlog was put in first, and shoved against the stones at the back wall. This section of wood was chosen carefully. It was a rather large log, 8-10 inches in diameter, from the best slow-burning trees, especially hard maple, hickory, or oak. Most importantly, it was green, unseasoned wood, with the bark left on, so that it burned only reluctantly. The main fire was built of dry, seasoned wood stacked in front of the big backlog. The massive backlog burned steadily, if exceedingly slowly, and so could last for days. All the while the drier logs arranged in front of it cracked and popped and flamed furiously – but they needed to be replaced several times a day. At night, the fire was banked, with the ashes and coals heaped up against the backlog. Up in the early morning, the husband or wife would stir the coals up away from the backlog and toss on some dry chips and twigs. The intense heat emanating from the backlog soon caused the whole to whoosh back into flame, and so the fire was started for a new day.

Thus, the backlog was a way to guarantee fire on the morrow. If you think about it carefully, you'll see why the pioneers' backlogs and our modern backlogs have a lot in common. Modern backlogs always involve a slow burn, just like the pioneers' backlogs did, but the pioneers didn't have to take antacids to cool the fire! Seriously, a backlog was (and is) an assurance for the future, future delivery of goods or services for us twenty-first century-ites, fire for days to come for our pioneers.

Outfoxed

The loveliest animal I ever saw – on four legs, anyway – was a wild red fox sprinting away across a sunlit autumn hill like a bow-flung fire-arrow. Its back was the color of a reddish pumpkin, its tail a brush as long and thick as the rest of its body. Its delicate black-stockinged feet moved in a blur, yet it didn't seem to be running, but flowing, with power and grace I can't describe. It was long ago, in the mid-1950's. Joe Hays and I, two quail hunters, one young and one old, had by chance startled that fox out of a patch of weeds in front of us. We were as surprised as the fox, maybe more. We didn't even raise our shotguns, just watched, in awe, as the thing ran. The bird dogs didn't bother to chase it; they knew they were licked before they started. It was gone in seconds, but the sight of it nailed into my memory.

There it lingers, half a century later, like a silent videotape. I play that tape when my spirits are drooping and I need to be heartened by the thought of something beautiful and graceful and wild.

For some mysterious reason foxes long ago captured our fancy. Maybe it's because they are so darned smart, or so nimble and beautiful. They certainly have taught us many lessons. The moral of Aesop's tale of the fox and the grapes – known to all of us – is that we often come to despise something we want badly and can't get possession of, despite trying hard to get it. In the end we give up and say "sour grapes," declaring that the thing isn't worth having anyway. Aesop, an ancient Greek who spent time in the outdoors and knew foxes (and people) well, wrote at least a dozen different fables in which a fox was the key character. Aesop's fox once outsmarted a goat, using it as a stepladder to save himself from being trapped in a well. Another fox, after bragging to a cat about all the hundred ways he had to escape his enemies, was caught and ripped apart by a pack of hunting dogs because he couldn't decide which escape route to choose as the baying pack approached. The cat, not nearly so clever – it had only one strategy to escape danger – survived by climbing a tree. And so it was that Aesop's fox was often a bit too clever and too proud of its cleverness. In this regard it resembled some of Aesop's fellow citizens and neighbors (and ours).

Jim Schmitt, a friend of mine from long ago, told me that once he was walking on a path in the woods and came face to face with a big red fox. That fox, which had been trotting along the path towards him, saw Jim coming and promptly just stopped and sat down, fifty feet away. There he rested on his haunches; head high, his big yellow eyes with their cat-like slits watching Jim closely. This unnerved Jim more than a little. Foxes are supposed to run away from people, not sit down in front of them. Foxes that aren't afraid of people may have rabies, to which they are particularly susceptible. Not wanting to get any nearer to a possibly dangerous animal, Jim picks up a stick and heaves it at the fox. To Jim's amazement, the fox springs into the air and with two quick bounds reaches the stick – which had landed wide of its mark. He takes it crossways in its jaws, holds his head high and then runs joyfully back and forth, like a dog at play. Eventually he drops the stick, and settles down on his haunches again, watching Jim attentively. Jim flings another stick. The fox takes it in its jaws like before, running around with it like a playful puppy. The performance is repeated another time. Eventually the fox prances away into the woods, head high, the stick held in its jaws like a proud trophy. Jim swore that the fox must have once watched a man throwing sticks for a dog to fetch, and had decided that it would be fun to play that game if he ever got a chance. He did. And it *was* fun.

It's clear that foxes do have fun, do know what the French call joi de vivre, the delight in life. J. David Henry, a wildlife biologist, once watched a fox racing airplanes – not ordinary little single engine sport airplanes either, but big multi-engine jets. As he leaned back in his seat as his passenger jet waited for clearance to take off, he glanced out the window and saw a red fox at the edge of the runway, watching the airplane. It was snowing hard and a gale of flakes was driving horizontally down the runway. As the engines came up and the aluminum monster began its take-off roll, the fox began trotting alongside. As the jet rolled faster and faster, the fox began loping and then running hard into the wind-driven snow, its ears laid back. At first the fox pulled ahead, its big tail straight and buoyant, its head high and proud. Slowly the aircraft overtook the fox and it disappeared from Henry's view. Moments later, as the jet banked away, he saw the fox once again, now far below. He watched as it turned and loped back to its starting point, taking up its position beside the next jet, which had taxied into place and was waiting to take off.

Our Midwestern pioneer ancestors were well acquainted with foxes, both the red-coated variety as well as the rather shyer gray fox. The acquaintance of fox and pioneer was renewed with a degree of regularity. Usually this happened in the middle of the night when the slumbering head of the house, exhausted from chopping trees all day, was startled out of his forty winks by a caterwauling and squawking issuing from the chicken coop. The fox had come for his dinner and the chickens – also invited – protested vociferously. Usually by the time the unhappy defender of his Sunday dinner arrived on the scene, the fox was already trotting away over the ridge with a fat pullet in his jaws. The cluck-clucking, squalling and squawking cacophony that announced the visit of the fox left an indelible impression on the minds of our beloved pioneers. Nothing was worse than "putting the fox in the chicken coop." Not only was there a predictable ear-splitting uproar, the goose of the chickens was pretty much cooked.

And so the fox has crept into our language. A clever fellow pioneer, adept at deviously gaining his ends, was considered as sly as a fox – not an entirely complimentary description. A fleet-footed youngster could run like a fox. Anyone who was outwitted in a game, or in business, or even in war, had been outfoxed. Francis Marion, one of the genuine heroes of the American Revolution, was adept at attacking the British seemingly out of nowhere. He then disappeared into the marshes and flooded lowlands of South Carolina as quickly as he came. The British came to call him "The Swamp Fox." It was a term of highest respect.

Over a Barrel

Barrels, especially big hand-made wooden ones built of oak staves held together with inch-wide steel bands, have pretty much disappeared from our lives. The closest thing to a wooden barrel we see these days is the wooden planter we purchase at the garden center. We proudly put it on our veranda or front porch and fill it with petunias to display our good taste. It's the remnant of a whisky barrel that has outlived any usefulness in its original role, whereupon it was sawed in half and given a new mission in life, namely as a container of a things of beauty, i.e., posies and garden gnomes.

Otherwise we just don't hear much about barrels anymore. There is, though, one glaring exception: we hear on the news every day the latest price of a barrel of crude oil. It strikes me that most of us have no idea how much a barrel actually holds – 64 gallons. If we conjure up an image of those (ever-more-expensive) barrels of oil we probably make a mental picture of chest-high, cylindrical metal drums. It's a little funny that even today we talk daily about barrels of oil when people haven't put crude oil in actual barrels since the days of John D. Rockefeller. They have long since been supplanted by oil pipelines and railroad tank cars.

I love wooden barrels, for a dozen reasons. In the first place, they are commonly built of oak. What wood can you think of that has a better reputation for strength, durability and even beauty? Didn't your ancestors arrive at Jamestown and Plymouth Rock in wooden boats? Boats built of which wood? Oak, of course, not balsa wood or knotty pine! And as your hoary ancestors rode the waves westward to the shores of America in their buoyant oaken vessels, what did they eat? Pickled beef and molasses and hard-tack and apples, etc., all stored safely in what? – oaken barrels. And what did those folks drink? Beer, and wine, and even water (only when the beer and wine were gone, of course), from oaken casks. Without those oaken containers your honored forebears would have starved to death or died of thirst en route. And where would *you* be then? Not reading this essay, that's for sure. So are oaken barrels important to you? Of course!

Barrels are *useful*, or once were, a trait we Americans admire almost excessively, sometimes to the detriment of ornamental things. "Useful" is American, ornamental is European at best and Oriental at worst. We carry our esteem of usefulness to the point where we see a farm tractor or a manufactured house as a thing of beauty. Looked at in this way, barrels have it, don't they?

Wooden barrels are more than useful, they are durable. That glass of fine highland malt whisky that warms your soul (and tummy) on a frosty winter evening took on *its* soul by melding with the charred interior of an oaken barrel for 10 or 15 years, or even longer. Can you imagine what that whisky would taste like if it were stored for a decade or two in a plastic barrel? Yuk!

Wooden barrels are (or once were) indispensable articles of commerce and war. One of the more remarkable characters ever (yes, I mean *ever*) was Sir Francis Drake. He's now largely forgotten by the general public because they don't make movies about him any more. The general public (i.e., us) now cares far more for home runs hit by steroid-assisted baseball giants or for the bullet-like 60-yard passes of filthy-rich football players than it does for actual heroes like Drake, a man who merely risked his life and saved civilization for ... for ... the benefit of modern sports fans who worship steroid-athletes and support their vast salaries by watching them play on TV and buying the stuff hawked during the (seemingly endless) commercials.

Anyway, Sir Francis' knowledge of barrels and barrel-making was the reason that the fight between the Spanish Armada and the English Navy occurred in 1588 instead of 1587. And his knowledge of barrel staves was the reason the English triumphed. 'Tis true. Read on.

Drake began his career as a freebooter and pirate in the 1570's, making a name for himself by swashbuckling across the Spanish Main. He was such an able chap that Queen Elizabeth (the Virgin Queen) later sent him round the world in his ship, the Golden Hind. The Queen (who probably wasn't really a virgin but just followed the advice of her press agent), expected that Drake would smash the Spanish in their underbelly, gather up boatloads of gold and jewels, and maybe grab some more land for Merrie Olde England. Indeed, Drake returned three years later, in 1581, in high triumph. He handed the Queen fistfuls of gold and jewels taken from Spanish ships as expected, and presented her double-handfuls of new English lands to boot. All this caused Elizabeth to smile broadly and tap Francis' shoulders with a dull sword, after which everyone, Queen included, called him "Sir."

There was a good reason that Sir Francis' stock rose so high: he was frightfully smart. In 1587, when word seeped into England that the evil Spanish were hard at work building a giant armada in which to come up and whip the English butts, Drake pondered the situation, drew on his vast encyclopedia of practical seafaring knowledge, and hatched the perfect plan to disable the enemy fleet: He would attack and destroy the Spanish staves.

Yes, you read that right: "attack and destroy the Spanish staves."

Let me explain: Drake knew that sailors had to eat and drink. Hungry and thirsty sailors – especially those without their snort of rum before a battle – didn't fight worth a damn. He knew that all the food and drink the swabs wolfed down at sea came out of wooden casks or barrels. Smart as he was, the brilliant Drake also knew that a bad barrel wouldn't hold water (or beer or rum or anything liquid, for that matter). He knew, as well, that good barrels (or, for that matter, casks, butts, firkins, hogsheads, kilderkins, pens and pipes) had to be built using well-seasoned staves. Let me explain further: after being cut into the proper shapes, barrel staves were kept outside in the sun and the rain for several years. Only then, after many cycles of rain-washing, sun-drying, freezing, swelling, shrinking, expanding and contracting, were they ready to be fitted into a barrel. If unseasoned staves were used, the barrel (cask, etc.) leaked. That led to problems, of course: kegs of soggy gunpowder, gooey messes on the deck and in the ship's hold, rotten fruit, stinking pork, omitted rum rations for the Limeys and most importantly, grumbling, cantankerous sailors who talked back to their officers and fought like feeble Aunt Sally.

In early 1787 Drake's spies brought thrilling news: the Spanish hoard of staves being seasoned for use with the a-building armada were at Cape St. Vincent in Portugal, at the southwestern-most point in Europe. Not a man to sit around and play pinochle, Drake and his men swooped in and burned the entire supply of seasoning staves, 1600 tons of them. As a result the Spanish were delayed by a year and forced to build containers for their armada out of half-seasoned wood. As you might have figured out by now (or maybe have read), they leaked, the food in them spoiled, and guess what? the Spanish armada was defeated. All of this... well, at least part of it... because Drake burned a pile of barrel staves. My point is that wooden barrels are of great importance – or at least once were.

I'm just old enough to remember an actual wooden barrel (I wish I weren't; it's more fun to be young and ignorant than old and wise). As I ponder that remembered barrel, the following vision comes into focus on my mental TV screen:

The year is 1952. Red-headed Larry Bledsoe's feet are off the ground because he is draped over the lip of a four-foot high wooden water barrel behind our neighbor Frank Jerrell's house on Second Street Northwest in Linton. Larry is 10 years old, like me. He's a nice guy, but gullible, a trait I take advantage of from time to time when I need amusement. I liked him, I did, especially when I needed protection from those roughnecks from West Linton, the Hobbs boys and the Hensleys. Larry was big for his age, taller and meatier than I, and not easily cowed. He was the kind of guy you wanted as a friend when you were in a fix. He maybe didn't run wind sprints between the earlobes, but his strength and size got respect.

I had persuaded Larry to take a close look at the mosquito wrigglers that swarmed in the crystal clear water. I loved to watch those insects when they came to the surface of the water in the barrel to get air. The water came to within a foot of the top. Larry was draped over the rim of the barrel, feet off the ground, his face within inches of the water surface. As I stood there contemplating Larry's broad posterior I grew exasperated at trying to explain to him for the third time what he was supposed to be seeing. Just then an evil spirit suddenly descended upon me. I bent down, grabbed his ankles and lifted. Larry easily slid head-first into that barrel of 3-feet deep rainwater with a splash and a glub. I was delighted momentarily as I watched his legs kicking frantically out the top of the barrel, but then it occurred to me that he might drown. I pushed the barrel over and saved his life, congratulating myself on my quick thinking and heroic spirit. I then ran for my life. Happily, I was always faster than he.

My affection for wooden barrels is embedded in my genes, I think, some of which were passed down to me by Wesley Fletcher Landrum (1827-1918), my great great grandfather. He was a cooper, that is, a barrel-maker. He got his start in that career because he grew up near the village of Freedom, in Owen County in southwestern Indiana. He lived there on the West Fork of the White River for much of his life. Freedom was an assembling point for flatboats that dropped down the White bound for New Orleans from the 1820's till after the Civil War – at which time the railroads came in and killed the boating business. Flatboats carried the farmers' excess produce down the river to New Orleans. These simple vessels were piled to the gunwales with casks of molasses, hogsheads of salted pork, and barrels of whisky. The boats never came back from New Orleans; they were sold along with their cargo, so new ones had to be built every year. Nor did the casks and barrels come back; they found buyers in the Southland as well. As a result, there was a steady demand for new wooden barrels and casks in Freedom, a need one-eyed Wesley labored mightily to fill.

In the first decades of the 1800's, barrel-making became a substantial industry in the booming Mid-west. In the 1830's, just as an example, the John Richards Steam Cooperage in Cincinnati, Ohio, employed 50 workers and annually manufactured 1,600 half-barrels, 34,000 pork barrels, 15,000 lard kegs, 4,000 hogsheads, and 1,000 tight hogsheads. Barrels were such a part of everyday life that people took them for granted. Words and phrases related to barrels naturally crept into our language.

Though the wooden barrels have now largely gone from our modern lives, those barrel-related words and phrases still linger on in our speech. You don't understand? Aha! I have you over a barrel. Believe me when I say that coming up with more examples is as easy as shooting fish in a barrel. I don't have to jump through hoops to do it, either. Next time you are barreling along in your giant SUV, don't succumb to road rage and make an obscene gesture at that guy in front of you. If he pulls over and climbs out of his car to confront you, you may discover that he is a barrel-chested bruiser. You may have to stand up to his attack and somehow stave him off. Nothing is as much fun as a barrel of monkeys, you'll have to admit. Politicians, whose main purpose in life is to get re-elected, try to please their constituents by pushing pork barrel legislation for their (and his) benefit. Some of those politicos are as crooked as a barrel full of snakes. Others, still more disreputable, are as crooked as a barrel of fish hooks. The worst of them are so crooked they can stand up in that barrel of fish hooks without getting stuck.

There's still more. In these days of gigantic food portions at fast-food places and restaurants, it's no surprise that many of the customers are as big as a barrel, and round as one, too. If you make a purchase deal in a shop, the modern seller may well refuse to take your credit card, demanding instead cash on the barrel head. Everyone knows that one bad apple can spoil a barrel full. A wise man knows never to fight with someone who buys ink by the barrel. When there is almost nothing left to choose from, all of us are left scraping the bottom of the barrel. In that case, dancing the beer barrel polka may help relieve the tension, especially if we remember to roll out the barrel first. Certainly, as the Russians say, an empty barrel makes the most noise. Irish folk wisdom teaches us that you can't build a barrel around a bung hole. Certainly someone who is really daring is willing to go over the falls in a barrel, which is more dangerous than barrel racing. Neither is more thrilling, perhaps, than riding in an airplane that does a barrel roll.

I'm finished with this essay and have run out of barrel terms, but I have to admit that writing it has been a barrel of fun.

Slept Like a Log

T rees were ponderous impediments for the early settlers who came to make their lives in the Ohio River Valley. To start with, they got in the travelers' way. Roads were terrible, not more than rambling tracks through the woods. Those roads were notorious for the obstacles they offered: mud holes in low places, fallen trees, stumps that grabbed the bottom of the wagon and stopped its progress, cut-off saplings that threatened to impale any careless traveler who tumbled off his precarious perch on his stumbling horse or plunging wagon. Such roads led far off into the woods and often forked and ended nowhere, too.

When your average early settler finally reached Indiana (or Ohio or Illinois or Wisconsin), he purchased Congressional land – land sold by the government for $1.25 per acre. He thereby acquired little more than the right to clear the "green timber," the pioneer term for virgin forest. His newly purchased woodlands were useless compared to corn lands – land laid bare of timber – corn land being in fact better than money in the bank (which is saying a lot, considering that our settler had no money and there were no banks).

The best thing our pioneer ancestors could do with trees was to turn them into logs and burn them or build with them. This they undertook with a vengeance. It was hard and dangerous work. The thock-thocking of the pioneer's axe was the very music of the pioneer land, its sound ringing up the hillsides and down the valleys. Each tree-chopper had his own tempo and the sound of his axe whacking into the wood of an oak or a yellow poplar had its distinctive timbre; when two or three axmen worked on the same tree they would fall into a marvelous rhythm: thock – thock- THOCK, thock – thock- THOCK, thock – thock- THOCK! It was a sound and a rhythm that moved on with the frontier, but is gone for most of a hundred years already, and gone forever. Nobody chops down trees any more. He uses a chain saw.

A good man with the axe could clear a few acres of ground each year, more if he had sons. By buying cheap Congressional land and transforming it into crop ground by chopping away the trees, a man could, slowly, over the years, become well-to-do – by the local standards of the day, anyway. No wonder men had a lot of children: they were a guaranteed supply of involuntary labor. The author's great great great grandfather, Joseph Landrum of Owen County, who came to Indiana from Halifax County, Virginia, in 1821, had fifteen children. As regards producing offspring he was fairly typical for that time and place, and certainly no record-setter. But oh, his poor wife!

The first logs, felled with a chopping axe and dragged to the home site by his team of horses, were stacked on top of one another to make the walls of his cabin. They were twenty feet long and trimmed flat, top and bottom with an adze, then notched on their ends by skilled use of the broad axe. After applying some clay and wood wedge chips for chinking, that stout log wall warded off the wind, snow and mosquitoes. The cabin roof was made of shingles split from straight-grained oak using a forgotten implement called a frow. One species of tree in the Midwest was so well suited for roofing that it took its common name from the use to which it was put: shingle oak. In better cabins the puncheon floor was made from split logs or thick planks smoothed on their upper surfaces with a foot adze. The door was of puncheon, too, hung on metal hinges if there was a blacksmith in the neighborhood, but leather was often used, especially in the earliest days when no blacksmith was available to make iron ones. With primitive implements and a lot of sweat a man with skill and strength could build a strong, tight, warm cabin using not a single nail.

Abraham Lincoln – whose boyhood in Spencer County, Indiana, was typical for a pioneer lad – had legendary skills with the axe. Thanks to a youth spent with that implement, he grew to have enormous physical strength which he retained to the end of his life. During the Civil War, when he was already a relatively old man, he attended the test firing of some new weapons in the vicinity of Washington, D.C. After the tests were complete, Lincoln spied an axe laying nearby. Picking it up, he remarked to the officers gathered around him that when he was a young fellow he had the strength to grasp the end of the three-foot handle with one hand and hold the axe out at arms length parallel to the ground. To the amazement of the on-lookers (and to Lincoln himself) he found he was still able to perform this feat – all the more remarkable considering Lincoln's long arms and advancing years. Men being men, one young officer after another had a try at it while Lincoln looked on. None of them could manage. Abe Lincoln, the wood chopper and rail splitter who just happened to be President of the United States, had a good chuckle.

Another President, William Henry Harrison, owed his election to a log cabin – a fictitious one, in fact. As the campaign for the Presidency warmed up in the summer of 1840, the Whig political handlers of the day cast about for a way to help voters identify with their candidates – Harrison and John Tyler, both originally from Virginia. Recognizing the virtues of pioneer life – of men and women triumphing over poverty and adversity while making a successful life in the awakening land – they could think of nothing more appealing than associating their candidates with the log cabin. Thus began the "Log Cabin and Hard Cider" campaign. "Tippecanoe and Tyler too" was the campaign slogan – recalling Harrison's victory over the Shawnees at the Battle of Tippecanoe 29 years earlier. Posters and newspaper stories pictured Harrison sitting on the stoop of his log cabin with a cup of hard cider in his hand. The picturesque message was that he was just a common man, living in a simple, virtuous log dwelling and drinking hard cider, the poor man's drink – not those sissy imported French wines. Voters of that day could identify with such a candidate, and they elected him with a good majority. The irony was that Harrison had never in his life lived in a log cabin. He was, in fact, a silver spoon aristocrat born to a prominent Virginia family. Clearly, we of the twenty-first century weren't the first to invent political fictions to get candidates elected.

The logs our beloved pioneers produced were so much a part of their lives that the very word "log" worked its way deep into our language. It still lodges there. Who hasn't slept like a log? Or, for that matter, slept poorly and woke up feeling loggy? Which of us hasn't sat daydreaming in class at school, only to be awakened from our reverie by an annoyed teacher who accused us of sitting there like a bump on a log? At that moment we probably felt dumb as a stump. Everyone knows – probably from experience – that nothing is easier than falling off a log. Politicians still make stump speeches – the stumps being the part remaining after the log had been removed. They know that it is essential to help other politicians in order to be helped by them in return – in other words, he understands about log rolling. Log rolling is a term that harks back to the days

when men from the entire neighborhood assembled to help a neighbor roll the logs he had felled into piles for burning, and so to finish clearing a patch of land.

Making logs from tree trunks required prodigious chopping of course, and the flailing axe produced a blizzard of wood chips. The determined woodchopper was often so intent in finishing a log quickly that he was oblivious to the flying wood chips, and so he let them fall where they may. If a son was as good with the axe as the father, his dad was proud to say that the youngster was a chip off the old block. Wood chips were everywhere in the early days of settlement, and so, when rowdies gathered to drink pioneer whisky (or hard cider) and boast about their prowess as fighters, it was the custom to challenge all comers by putting a wood chip on one's shoulder and daring anyone to knock it off. Someone spoiling for a fight today still has a chip on his shoulder. Late in pioneer days, logs were hauled to mills to be sawn into planks on ponderous, unsprung wagons drawn by teams of oxen or mules. These clumsy vehicles were notoriously difficult to manage and gave a jarring ride. Today, when we try to maneuver a clumsy automobile or truck down the road and manage to do so only with difficulty, we still say that the vehicle drives like a log wagon. Of course, log wagons have been gone from Indiana for the better part of a century but for some reason we are still driving them.

Hog Wild

Surely the ugliest of all animals for sophisticated folks like you and me is the common hog – also known as pig, swine, porker, boar or sow, among others.

[At this point lightning flashes and thunder sounds offstage: Your mustachioed reader continues, sweeping his arms in a grand gesture and pointing to his left:]

Here, ladies and gentlemen, astonishingly, thanks to the miracle of prestidigitation, stands one of that species right here before us, ready for us to inspect. Join me in a closer look.

First, I direct your attention to its repulsive snout projecting like a stunted elephant trunk out over its leering mouth. Next, contemplate its beady little eyes. Observe that they watch us closely,

like a criminal or a weasel, suspicious and mean. And then please note those pointy, floppy ears that look like flaps of scar tissue. Now, dare – if you will – to touch its back. Go ahead! You feel the repulsive bristles, thick, coarse and pointy, don't you? They are rough and somehow greasy. I don't wonder that you quickly draw back your hand. Take a step away now and notice how thick and cylindrical the brute is, how it is slung low to the ground like a fatty sausage. And see there hanging off its rounded rump the preposterous short corkscrew of a tail. How useless and ridiculous it is! Finally, observe the animal's off-putting attitude toward us. It beady-eyes us in its disdainful pig-like way as if to say "get out of my life."

It's no wonder that the more delicate souls among you may think of the common porker with genteel revulsion and even suffer a little involuntary shudder.

Surely the only creature that could love a hog is another hog.

Not true! Our pioneer ancestors loved 'em.

Strange to say, hogs were not ugly in the eyes of those hardy people, but the very opposite – lovely. To them the thought of a hog or a pig could evoke a smile, at least an inner one. The sound of squealing piglets and oinking sows was veritable music. The smell of hog manure was the scent of money. The sight of a fat sow conjured up the prospect of a steaming, mouth-watering pork roast, and of a well-fed family. Yes, a mid-western pioneer farmer with a fine drove of hogs roaming in the woods around his log cabin was *rising* in the world.

Wait! Hogs roaming in the woods? Yes, in fact! Until the widespread penetration of barbed wire into the Mid-west in the late

1800's, hogs roamed wild in the woods. Free-range porkers thrived because ordinary rail or wire fences could not keep them from going where they wanted to go and doing what they wanted to do. Mostly, this amounted to soaking in a cool, self-made mud wallow in the heat of a summer day and rooting for worms and acorns in the woods at night. Pioneer hogs were pretty much wild. The free-spirited wandering porker was invariably spooked by the sight of man (or boy) because he had learned early in his life to expect little from humankind except trouble.

Logan Esarey, the Hoosier historian, born in 1873, wrote an endearing account of life in early Indiana. He captured the details of everyday life in the heyday of his Indiana pioneer grandparents in the 1850's. None of my words can describe the importance of the hog better than Professor Esarey:

"We may sing the praises of all the heroes of Indiana from LaSalle or George Rogers Clark to the present, but the prosperity of our state through the [nineteenth] century has depended on Mr. Hog."

Prosperity depending on the hog? How was this?

In the first place, hogs fed the pioneer family, and fed them well. Fall was hog slaughtering time, in late November or early December. By then the weather was cool enough that meat wouldn't spoil quickly.

A few weeks before slaughter the farmer would leave a pile of ear corn near the spring where the hogs came to drink – to fatten them up. And he would gradually get them accustomed to feeding at a trough set up not far from the house. On this he would leave some rotten potatoes or bad apples or sour milk. This fattening added sweetness to the already thick layer of lard the hogs had acquired by feeding on the abundant mast – beech nuts, acorns, and American chestnuts. One type of nut the wild hogs readily consumed was one that the pioneer family didn't bother with because the nutmeats were so small. The pignut, a species of hickory, took its name from the hogs themselves.

Rounding up the hogs in the fall for slaughter required the whole family and sometimes neighbors coming over to help. Hooting and shouting and beating on pans they drove the squalling beasts from their distant woodland haunts into a waiting pen. There the younger pigs were separated from the slaughter hogs and notches cut in their ears to identify them as belonging to a particular family. These notches were legal proof of ownership and each man's mark was registered at the county courthouse for reference when there was a dispute. And many a dispute there was. Hogs, ranging far and wide in the unfenced country, frequently ended up on another man's property, and often enough in that fellow's pig pen. County courts

regularly heard lawsuits over the ownership of a particular pig; sometimes the charge was that the accused had deliberately changed one man's crop mark into his own – an early version of rustling. The crime – if actual crime there was – is perhaps understandable, given how poor people were then, and the fact that a fat hog was worth a whole dollar!

Like many pioneer activities in which neighbor helped neighbor – the cabin raising, the log rolling, the husking bee – hog butchering was a pitch-in affair. Men, wives and children from the neighborhood roundabout would arrive, in high spirits, with their butcher knives, whetstones and sundry pots, ready for work. After the roundup, the hogs were shot in the head, then hung up from a convenient tree limb and bled by slitting the jugular vein. Sometimes the heart was still beating when the cut was made, and blood came gushing out in crimson spurts. The carcass was plunged into a vat of boiling water until the hair and bristles came loose. Then the entire hog was scraped clean, after which it was gutted, the innards plopping into a clean oaken tub. The heart and liver were sliced out and hung up for quick consumption while the brains were scooped out for frying. Some of these sweetmeats – which, in the days before refrigeration, wouldn't keep – were carried home by the neighbors as a reward for their help. The head – ears, tongue, lips and all – was cut off and boiled until the meat fell away from the bones. After dicing the meat and fat into cubes and adding pepper and spices, the whole concoction was allowed to congeal into a jellied brei called head cheese, or souse.

Butchering proceeded, resulting in slabs of fatback bacon, shoulders and big hams, all of which were liberally rubbed with salt and hauled off to the smokehouse to be dried and cured over hickory smoke. Smoked meat would keep for months without refrigeration. Slabs of fat were thrown into big iron pots for rendering into lard – the only cooking fat that people knew in those days. The skins with meat and fat still attached were fried into cracklings, which had a sweet, meaty flavor.

The ribs were chopped off with the help of a mallet and chisel or a hatchet, and the leftover bones cleaned of meat.

Every helper family carried home a sack of bones to flavor the common man's fare of boiled beans and cornbread. The pigs feet and knuckles were used, too, either pickled in vinegar or boiled to make a meaty soup. The stomach was washed and filled with the congealed blood to make bloodwurst, a kind of sausage. The intestines were used too. Turned inside out, washed and scraped and filled with chopped meat and fat, they made juicy sausages. If the unfortunate slaughtered hog was a boar, his enormous testicles were not neglected either.

In those days of hardship and poverty, hog slaughtering was a time of happiness and abundant, delicious food. The hog gave his all for it, literally, every last part of him, except maybe the squeal.

In the course of an average week the pioneer family table was the gathering place for a long list of pork-based delights. For breakfast, eggs fried in lard were inevitably served up accompanied by strips of sugar-cured bacon or sausage. When the farmer set off to his fields amornings for a long day of plowing or cultivating his corn, he might carry a sack of cracklings, which didn't need to be kept cold. Or he might tote a slice of smoked ham wedged between slabs of home-baked bread. Dinner that night offered the famished woodchopper or plowman a pork loin, pork chops, pork ribs, pork fritters or a nicely browned pork roast. In the course of the year when the smokehouse larder grew bare, it was time to eat salt pork – steeped in brine for many months. There might be pickled pigs feet, or cuts of head cheese that had been preserved in the spring house, or fried "mountain oysters," a euphemism for cooked testicles. Fried brains – eaten soon after slaughter since there was no freezer to preserve them – were considered by some to be mouth-watering good.

Hogs gave more than food to the pioneer. Excellent hair brushes were made with hog bristles. Fine leather goods, shoes, gloves, jackets, and vests, were fabricated from the grainy, tough hog hides. It's debatable, of course, whether a silk purse was ever made out of a sow's ear. But certainly hog fat was the basis of lye soap, made by boiling wood ashes with lard. The author remembers the 1950's, when Dellie Brock, born in 1878, daughter of the hills of Martin County, Indiana, still made her own lye soap, declaring that it washed the clothes a lot better than store-bought soap.

Professor Esarey justly celebrated the contribution of hogs to the Indiana economy. Beginning in the 1820's and lasting till the Civil War, flatboats carried the produce of tens of thousands of Indiana farms down its tributaries to the Ohio, whose currents swept the clumsy boats on their leisurely way to the Mississippi and on to New Orleans. Barrels of salt pork were often the cargo, sometimes even hogsheads of it. For the first fifty years or so of the nineteenth century, large herds of hogs reached the Ohio by a different route. They were driven from central Indiana and Ohio to Cincinnati, Ohio – called for a time "Porkopolis," or to Madison, Indiana, where pork processing plants processed countless tons of pork for the eastern markets.

It's no wonder that words and phrases associated with hogs became part of the pioneer vocabulary; they linger on in our speech today. What modern teenager, for example, wants to be as fat as a hog

– even though, in these calorie-rich fast food days, she has plenty of company. She and her boyfriends obviously spend too much time pigging out. Many of them look like they have been living high on the hog and as a result have become as fat as pigs. In the local teen hangout – likely a fast-food joint – she and her buddies feel like they are in hog heaven. Given a sandwich, a mayonnaise jar and a knife, they are likely to go hog wild and lard it on. Offered a tray of food they are liable to be observed hogging it.

At home the typical teenager – both of today and yesteryear – are likely to be accused by their parents of keeping their rooms looking like a pigsty. Or a hog wallow. Ordered to clean up his room, the young man is liable to slip away from his duty as slick as a greased pig. This curious term "greased pig" harks back to pioneer days when a pig was basted with lard and set free for the boys to catch – the pig being the prize. The hilarity that ensued had the pioneers holding their sides. Today, if a boy is rebellious, he may exclaim in a shrill voice that yes, he'll clean up his room, in a pig's eye! He'll likely stride out of the house as mad as a wild boar. Which of us hasn't sweated like a pig, especially after it dawns on us that we

stupidly bought a pig in a poke? And who among us hasn't cut himself so badly that he bled like a stuck hog?

Even the politicians haven't avoided the hog scene. For these worthies, pork barrel legislation – to benefit the home constituency while the vaunted balanced budget be damned – is still extremely popular, especially for the public servant who wants to be reelected. And which of them doesn't? It seems a grand irony that the only pork barrels left today are being rolled by politicians – at a time when pork itself hasn't been put in barrels for at least a century. So much for innovation in politics.

Too Many Irons in the Fire

enry Wadsworth Longfellow was long an icon among American poets, beloved by a wide public. Nostalgic Americans of the late 19th and first half of the 20th century revered him. He conjured up visions of the disappearing America they had known in their youths, or thought they remembered. I can still recall my father, in the late 1940's, sitting in his easy chair with his kids gathered around him, reading aloud to us in his rhythmical monotone:

> "By the shores of Gitchee-Gumee,
> By the shining big-sea water,
> Stood the wigwam of Nokomis ..."

I don't have to look up those words from Longfellow's Hiawatha, I *remember* them. They were drilled into my brain by repetition. Any of Dad's kids who failed to listen respectfully (or tried to slip away unnoticed) faced the prospect of the back of his hand. And he had big Scottish hands.

Anyway, Longfellow had a genius for picking nostalgic topics for his verses, and for writing wonderful, picturesque first lines:

> "Under a spreading chestnut tree
> The village smithy stands..."

Gee, you can almost hear the ringing of the blacksmith's hammer and see the red-glowing horseshoe on which he is banging away.

Trouble is, Henry Longfellow was like a sprinter who leaps gracefully out of the chocks when the starting gun fires, then stumbles and falls on his face.

For example, going on with the above first lines on the village smithy – which, by the way, inspired a wonderful painting:

"The smith a mighty man is he,
With large and sinewy hands,
And the muscles of his brawny arms
Are strong as iron bands."

You get the idea. A mighty man? Iron bands? Longfellow's versifying immediately goes down in a heap, overblown and clunky. You suspect that the poet would have been real good at hammering round pegs into square holes.

Not only that, Mr. Longfellow soon loses track of his blacksmith's whereabouts, even in a short effusion like this. Later in the poem, children come by on their way home from school and peek in the smithy door to watch him work. Wait! I thought he was outside under the spreading chestnut tree?

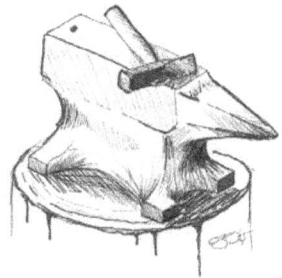

Oh well, one shouldn't be too critical.

Fact is, the village (or neighborhood) blacksmith was a valued member of every community. Anything made of iron he could make (or fix) with his skill and simple tools, namely hammers, tongs, anvil, fire and bellows. You name it: horseshoes, andirons, nails, door hinges, bootjacks, chains, pothooks, knives, scythes, and a great many more. He could make it.

Maybe with his subject blacksmith having so much business it was no wonder that Longfellow felt compelled to lather on the praise:

"His brow is wet with honest sweat,

He earns whate'er he can,

And looks the whole world in the face,

For he owes not any man."

Undoubtedly feeling under so much pressure to stay out of debt, Longfellow's blacksmith sometimes tried to get ahead by placing a number of objects in the forge to heat up at the same time, maybe a horseshoe, a hinge-half, a plowshare, a buckle, a clevis pin, a crowbar, etc. Unfortunately, iron takes a long time to heat up to the temperature at which it can be hammered. And if it gets too hot it can lose its shape or temper, and even burn. Our smithy couldn't waste time doing just one thing at a time. But he had to be careful to keep his mind on his work.

Inevitably, he would fall behind. Maybe it was because his thoughts were diverted by a poem he was composing, or more likely, because a neighbor stopped by to chat. Eventually, after being immersed in this diversion, he suddenly would start, leap out of his conversation with his visitor, spring to the forge, grab a burning piece of iron and fling it in the quenching tub. When the sizzle and the cloud of steam dissipated his visitor would inevitably ask: "What's wrong?"

"Too many irons in the fire!" he would reply.

Where the Wild Goose Goes

At some point in our early childhood the melodies and words of the popular songs of the day begin to scratch faint tracks in our memories. It's little short of astonishing that forty years or even eighty years later, those traces laid down in our childish brains are still there, though we may not have thought of them for decades of years.

There is a cryptic magic in those nearly-but-not-quite-forgotten tunes, magic in those almost-lost words and memories, though we call them to mind ever so rarely.

Stop for a moment, if you will, and think on *your* first memories of popular music. What are the first lyrics you remember, what are the first tunes that you can still sing, or at least just hum? Likely you can't recollect an entire song, but merely some partial chorus of it, some snatch of words which have slept there in your cranium for years and years like a buried railroad track. Wipe off the earth that covers it, rub away the rust, and tell me what you find.

Of course, only *you* can say what antique song memories you still carry around between your ears.

But I can tell you mine.

Here it is: Don't laugh! "Bongo Bongo Bongo I don't want to leave the Congo, No No No No No!"

Ok Ok! You may chortle at my silly memory, but allow me to remind you that I was barely five years old when that song became popular in the fall of 1947. It was the kind of ditty a little kid would like, of course. The Andrews Sisters warbled it, accompanied by Danny Kaye. At the time I didn't know what "Bongo" meant (I still don't) and I had no idea where the Congo was (I do now), but I knew darn sure I didn't want to leave it!

Another 1947 pop tune comes to my ear after nearly 60 years of forgetfulness, too, also a silly one: "Open the Door Richard, Richard why don't you open the door?" This one, like Bongo Bongo, never made the public all-time hits list but it is an all-time hit with me nevertheless, though I can't recall the name of the singer.

A singer I do remember, namely Frankie Laine, belted out a love song in 1949 that touched my little boy's heart:

"My heart knows what the wild goose knows.
I must go where the wild goose goes.
Wild goose, brother goose, which is the best,
A wanderin' heart or a heart at rest?"

That Song of the Wild Goose, its words, its evocative mystery of a distant bird winging away north following who knows what compass to places unknown, thrilled me, transported me beyond time and place. It was simply magic. It is magic still. Its lyrics touched on loneliness and love and the crossroads we come to in life, for which the wild goose was a perfect metaphor. Yes, I was far too young to grasp all of this at the time, but I was nevertheless transfixed.

One thought leads to another. Memory takes me back to an evening in my hometown of Linton, long ago. It is late October and Indian summer is upon us. I'm sitting on the front porch of Joe Hays' house on Second Street. Joe is smoking a Pall Mall, and I'm whittling on a stick. There is a light chill and the sun has gone down half an hour before but in the western sky it is still light among the splotches of dark clouds. We aren't talking, Joe and I, just thinking about things in our own way. We are true friends and don't need to talk all of the time.

"Listen," Joe suddenly says.

I turn my head, cocking an ear. At first I hear nothing, but I keep trying.

"Hear it?" Joe says.

I didn't, though I knew Joe wouldn't be joshing me. I strained to hear what he was hearing.

And then there it was, just barely audible, a sound as plaintive and lonesome as anything I ever heard, a faint "Ah-honk, Ah-ronk, Ah-honk."

It was the calling of geese, a kind of far-away music.

We listened for a while.

Joe said, "It's Canada geese, heading south for the winter." There was a tone in his voice that told me he was in awe of that sound, just as I was.

After listening for a minute, I asked, "Where are they going?"

"Nobody knows but them. Maybe Texas or Louisiana or the marshes of the Mississippi delta. Come on, let's go look if we can see 'em," Joe says.

We walked around the corner of the house and stopped where we could look to the west between the trees. There, in a patch of open sky in the eye-straining distance was a long line of Canada geese, three dozen dark spots lined up in a vee, one leg of it longer than the other, its point directed to the south. We watched that wavering line as it crawled southward in the distance. We saw half a dozen birds drop away from the long end of the main line, which grew more ragged for a minute as if there was momentary consternation in the ranks. The stragglers kept formation and eventually closed the gap. That line of geese acted as if it was itself a living thing.

"They're headin' south for the winter," Joe said.

"How do they know they should go south?" I asked.

"Mother Nature," Joe says. "She teaches 'em. The goose out on the point is the oldest and the wisest. It may be a gander, or a mother goose. Whichever it is, it takes the lead because it's done it many times, twenty or thirty times, year after year. It remembers the landmarks and follows the rivers and its instinct."

"Listen to that sound, son, and remember it. The geese talk to one another. Nobody knows what they are saying, for sure, but probably they are givin' one another encouragement, or keepin' discipline or makin' jokes about stragglers to shame 'em back into line. Probly some of them are complaining that they are tired, or hungry, and are tellin' the leader to drop down to that lake or river below so they can have a snack or a rest. Nobody knows but the wild geese themselves."

Joe paused for a moment. He had a distant look in his eyes.

"One thing about them wild geese, son, they make me envious, they stir me up somehow, make me want to go to faraway places, maybe. How about you?"

I admitted it did (and it still does).

Joe and I stood there in the late evening light as the sound of the geese faded and their ragged vee slipped out of sight behind some distant trees.

What Joe and I watched that evening in Linton long ago had been seen by millions of eyes long before that. Geese were a part of peoples' lives for hundreds of centuries before there were written records. The earliest human memories of geese were those of the primitive hunter-gatherers of twenty or forty thousand years ago.

Those stone age people undoubtedly marked the coming of winter and the return of spring by watching (and hearing) the migrations of the wild geese. Geese came to be symbols of perseverance, able, as they were, to undertake long, difficult journeys. They became symbols of aggressiveness, too, which you can easily test for yourself if you have the gumption for it: walk boldly up to a goose sitting on her nest of eggs. She will eye you warily as you approach, and begin to hiss, and as you get too near she will explode all over you, flogging you with her big wings and pecking and biting you with her big bill. You will scamper away to safety, I guarantee.

Some ten thousand years ago geese were domesticated, and over the following millennia goose lovers created dozens of breeds: the Sebastopol goose from southeastern Europe, the Chinese goose, the Toulouse, the Roman tufted, and many more. Geese became popular because they proved awfully useful to keep around. They produced big, nutritious eggs. Their down was extremely light and very warm and served for pillows and comforters against the cold nights in the primitive hovels, and in the palaces, too, of the day. Roast goose, nicely browned and dripping with sweet juices, was a delectable meal, fit for kings and common folk alike.

Geese were useful to have around for other reasons as well. In the year 390 B.C., Rome was laid siege by a barbarian Celtic army. It was a dark day for the fledgling Roman republic. Again and again the surviving Romans had been forced to retreat by the invading Celts. They found their last refuge at the top of Capitoline Hill. Detachments of soldiers with vicious guard dogs watched the valley approaches to this last sanctuary. No one bothered to watch the steep cliffs at their backs that surrounded the rest of the hill. They were thought impassable. The Celts knew otherwise. Early one morning they sent a party of warriors to scale the cliffs. As Celtic heads began popping up over the edges of the precipice, a flock of geese – kept nearby because geese were sacred to the God Juno, whose temple was on the hill – spotted them and raised a ruckus, hissing and honking. The noise alerted the Roman defenders, whose backs had been to the cliffs. They rushed in and threw the Celts over the precipice to their deaths. After that, geese were celebrated in a strange Roman ceremony in which they were carried through the streets on litters, a high honor. The geese were paraded past dogs that had been crucified, a punishment meted out because they had failed to bark and warn the defenders.

The moral of the story is that geese are better watchdogs than watchdogs. Their talent as sentries undoubtedly stems from the goose's social nature. When a flock of geese is feeding, one of them always stands guard. Though they are good flyers, geese, being big and slow, take quite a while to get airborne. The honking of the sentinel alerts the whole flock to the danger; they echo it with a great chorus of honks, which alone may be enough to scare off a nervous predator. But in any case the guard-goose gives the rest of the birds ample time to start goose-stepping and wing-flapping into their take-off run.

Geese were useful for other purposes as well, including play. The game of badminton is played with a shuttlecock, which flies gracefully back and forth over the net (except when I am playing). Few people know that the true shuttlecock (not the cheapo plastic one you buy at the drugstore) is made with 16 feathers, all taken from the left wing of a goose. The goose also figures largely in an old game played in the snow: Fox and Geese, and in another schoolyard game beloved by millions: Duck, Duck, Goose.

With the goose so much a part of our lives, many goose-related phrases and old saws have worked themselves into our daily speech. Anyone who has ever plucked a goose knows what the pink skin of the bird actually looks like, though I suspect that probably not one person in ten thousand today has ever actually plucked a goose. Nevertheless, probably every last one of us has been chilled, thrilled or terrified at one time or another, whereupon we declared that we had goose bumps (or goose flesh). There's another kind of goose swelling, the goose egg you get when your playmate accidentally whacks you on your cranium with a baseball bat. Both goose eggs and goose bumps are temporary, happily.

Perceptive people have noticed that geese are much better at walking than ducks, though neither can be described as graceful afoot. That's because ducks have their feet attached toward the rear of their bodies, and so are forced to waddle. Geese, by contrast, have longer legs, which are attached much further forward, making them capable of straight-away striding. Close inspection reveals that they kick their legs pretty-well out in front of them as they go, a feature that enamored them to Hitler and Mussolini. Those jut-jawed dictators required their parading legions to imitate the high-striding goose-step. For some reason the goose-step ceased to be popular after World War II.

Mother Goose is a beloved figure; her rhymes are drilled into the minds of children. You deny it? How about "Hickory, dickory, dock ..." or "Jack be nimble, Jack ..." or "Little Jack Horner sat in a corner ..."? One will get you ten than you can recite each of these rhymes by heart – where would you be without Mother Goose, anyway? She's part of your life and you will share her with your own children as well – if you haven't already done so. We may have learned those rhymes when our mother read them to us by the light of a goose-neck lamp.

In school, some of us are dunces. After taking an arithmetic quiz with ten questions, we may see our score in red at the top of the page: a big goose egg – reminiscent of the outline of the thing that drops out of a goose's bottom. That's what we feel like, too, when we see our score, a goose's bottom. In fact, the teacher may then call us a silly goose. When we get home to report the bad mark to our frowning father, we do so knowing that our goose is cooked. He's liable to tell us that we don't have the sense that God gave a goose. This is a bigger insult to us than it is to the goose.

All of us have gone on a wild goose chase. And when one of us sees something interesting, we pull on the sleeve of our companion, asking him to "take a gander at that." I wonder if that happens very often in Gander, Newfoundland? Goose-related old saws have worked their way into folklore. An Irish version – where the Yule goose is still quite popular as the centerpiece of the holiday feast – says that a goose never voted for an early Christmas. The Danes tell us that when the fox preaches to the goose his neck is in danger. And everyone knows that what is sauce for the goose is sauce for the gander. Of course something that passes through fast does so as slick as grass through a goose.

To shove hard on something – like the accelerator of a car – is to goose it. Goosing people – jabbing their posterior with a thumb and causing them to jump – was immensely popular in the '50's. Thankfully, this sort of social intercourse has fallen out of fashion. Pray that it doesn't come back.

A forgotten basketball hero of the mid-twentieth century was the Harlem Globe Trotter star, Goose Tatum, who got his name maybe because he was so loosey-goosey on the court. A famous baseball reliever was Goose Gossage. Goose Goslin, not related, was the sweet-hitting left fielder for the St. Louis Browns and the Washington Senators. He was the key to the only World Series victory the Senators ever claimed. He got his nickname from his beak-like nose and his gawky appearance – but opposing pitchers feared him, especially in clutch situations. Goslin said that if hadn't been for the difficulty he had seeing over his nose, he would have hit .500. I suppose all those guys were proud of their names – they were certainly distinctive, in any case.

I think I'll give up on this essay now, before I kill the goose that laid the golden egg.

Skinny as a Rail

The history of America is in her fences. Of course in the earliest days there were no fences at all, for Native Americans, with their free and roving life, had no need for them.

Everything changed when the Whites came. In early New England, where the only crop the plowed soil reliably produced was a harvest of rocks, the early farmers picked them up and stacked them atop one another and built walls to enclose their fields. By 1871, in tiny Rhode Island, for example, there were 14,000 miles of stone walls; the larger New England states had far more. Stone fence-building materials were right there at the farmers' feet, in the way, and had to be removed from the fields anyway, so they simply made the best of it. As the old saying goes, "if life gives you scraps, make quilts." For New England farmers the rocks were scraps and the fences were quilts.

To the south, in Pennsylvania and Virginia, and to the west, on the pioneer land in the Ohio River Valley being opened up to settlement, fences were built using another useless and in-the-way material: trees.

The trees were right there to hand, seemingly everywhere, of virtually no value, indeed, they represented impediments to progress and prosperity. Green timber land – the name given by our pioneer ancestors to old-growth forests – was far less valuable than cleared ground on which they could grow crops. The big trees had to be eliminated to plant corn, and so they were removed, mostly burned away in thousands of roaring pyres at pioneer community log-rollings, year after year. But the early mid-western farmers also made good use of some of the tree obstacles, using them to build fences, often of rails split out of honey locust or black walnut logs.

Those who first tamed the wilderness – the people of the frontier – built their fences to keep nature *out*, nature in those days being a hungry panther, a roving bear, or an Indian war party disputing the white man's right to settle on the land. Vertical log walls twelve or fourteen feet tall surrounded a cluster of frontier cabins, making up the fortified station. The station served as a refuge for outlying settlers who "forted up" when Indians were ravaging the countryside.

The early settlers' outlying cabins were always in clearings chopped out of the forest; they were surrounded by rail fences. Those spindly rail fences couldn't keep marauding Indians out, but they did hinder the cattle and the half-wild hogs, which wandered freely in the surrounding woods, from getting into the dooryard and eating the sweet corn and rooting up the vegetable garden. The pioneer farmer had to fence his cornfields, too, for the same reason, to keep the livestock out – the notion of fencing *in* the cattle and hogs and horses had not yet dawned on him. There was a practical economic reason for this: fenced-in livestock had to be fed, which required large feed or fodder stores and daily labor. Livestock roaming the river bottoms and up on the ridge, fed themselves.

In time, fences came to represent a measuring stick of progress, and thanks to the growing prosperity of the nineteenth century, rail fences were everywhere. Those fences had to be built, and repaired, of course. In pioneer days, in Indiana and other new midwestern states, young men commonly earned their money and sometimes their reputations by their skill with the axe, splitting rails. Young Abraham Lincoln's prowess with that implement became so legendary that later, when he campaigned for President in 1860, he was proudly advertised as "the Rail-splitter" from Illinois. The subtle message was that honest Abe was a common man who had done common work – that he was an ordinary guy – millions of voters identified with that.

Fence rails came to be so much a part of life of our pioneer ancestors that many related words and phrases came to be imbedded in our language and linger on in our speech today as unnoticed anachronisms. What American girl is not happy to be described as skinny as a rail, especially in these fat times when a more common description might be as thick as a barrel? What politician has not had a nightmare in which he was ridden out of town on a rail? And what public servant does not regularly return to his home precincts to slap the backs of his supporters and mollify the disgruntled ones, in other words, to mend his fences? The author's own grandfather once described something as being "as high as a nine-rail fence." And he heard his mother once describe a politician as "as crooked as a rail fence." To not commit oneself to one side or the other of a burning issue is "to sit on a rail," or "straddle the fence."

Yes, rail fences are gone forever, but in a very concrete way they are still very much with us.

A Flash in the Pan

The pioneer's rifle kept the wolf from the door and put meat on the table. It sometimes saved a man's life, and that of his women and children, too, when Indians attacked. Every pioneer family had one, and literally couldn't live without it. It was kept on pegs above the fireplace, dry and warm and in clear view and always ready when a deer, a panther, or an Indian, appeared unexpectedly in the cabin clearing. A glance at the rifle was always reassuring in the lonely cabin when, in the evening, the dogs sleeping by the hearth raised their heads and began growling ominously, or when something went thump against the cabin wall in the night.

Commonly built in Pennsylvania by meticulous German craftsmen, and accurate out to two hundred yards and more, the rifle was valued to a degree we can barely imagine today. Men had such affection for their rifles that they gave them names, usually female ones, and regarded them as their dearest friends.

Baynard Rush Hall, a highly-educated Easterner who, during the 1820's, lived several years in Indiana's "New Purchase" – land newly acquired from the Indians in 1818 – took powerful pride in his newly-learned skill as a marksman, for a peculiar reason: His prowess with the rifle won him respect from his neighbors, mostly uneducated folk from North Carolina and Kentucky. These people were otherwise suspicious of high-falutin' book-learned people like him. "The man can shoot!" they said.

Men would risk their lives for their favorite rifle. Hall tells the story of his uncle, whose affection for his firearm was heart-deep. Stranded once on an island in the Missouri River in winter as night came down, he attempted to swim the quarter-mile to shore while holding his rifle above the water with one arm. Freezing, exhausted, and in imminent danger of drowning, he let go his beloved weapon in a moment of weakness, felt it slip into the dark waters. Wild with despair at his loss, despite the extreme danger, he repeatedly dove down into the icy blackness and groped around the bottom in the hope of retrieving it, but in vain. Eventually, he struggled to the shore so exhausted he could barely drag himself out of the water. For a long time after that he was nearly inconsolable. Only by chance was he prevented from going back into the river to try to retrieve his beloved friend.

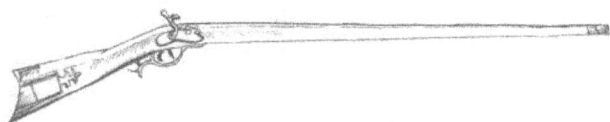

Rifles in those days were loaded from the muzzle with a charge of black powder, then the bullet, wrapped in a greased leather patch, was forced down the barrel with a ramrod. The firing mechanism involved a hammer that carried a flint at its tip, and the whole was cocked back with the thumb through two positions, half-cocked and fully cocked. When the trigger was pulled at full cock, the hammer was flung forward and the flint struck the frizzen, a metal surface. This caused a shower of sparks to fly onto the adjacent pan, a plate on which was sprinkled a charge of black powder. The charge ignited – the flash – whereupon the powder burned through a tiny port leading into the chamber which held the black powder behind the bullet. If all went well, that powder charge exploded, propelling the bullet along the barrel and out at high speed towards its target.

Sometimes the charge in the pan ignited but didn't burn down into the barrel. It merely flashed, with a sickening poof without the essential following bang. In other words, the gun didn't actually fire. This was the famous "flash in the pan." The marksman was left standing there with his rifle pointed at the target, totally frustrated. Hopefully he wasn't aiming at a panther ready to spring on him, or a prized 12-point buck. Hence, a flash in the pan was always an attention-getting but misleading, worthless and sometimes even dangerous event. Next time you declare something to be a flash in the pan, think about what it really means.

Till the Cows Come Home

What animal do we love more than any other or, rather, *should* we love more than any other?

I'm in earnest. It's a serious question. Give it some thought before you answer.

The *dog* you say? The animal with the lovely name *Canis familiaris?*

I admit that dogs are loveable. And if you had given me that dog answer a while back – say ten thousand years ago – I would have heartily agreed with you. But exactly what is it that dogs do for us *today* that is really, truly important? Think about it. I admit they support a large and lucrative dog food industry. And where would veterinarians be without them – starving! The answer to the "what do dogs do question" is "not much."

Admittedly dogs do make us feel good, from time to time, anyway. And yes, I am aware that they love us unconditionally – despite the fact that we may be fat or ugly – dogs are indifferent to our appearance, and adore us even if we look like gargoyles. Thousands of years ago master (or mistress) was lovingly adopted into their dog's own pack, and afforded honorary citizenship in dogdom in general, too. Dogs adopted us just as much as we adopted them. They were delighted to have us and we were happy to be loved as we truly (and sometimes repulsively) are – or think ourselves to be. And yes, still today, our dog's eyes sparkle and she wags her tail when she sees us coming, even when she is ailing and can barely stand. What is more pathetic and heartwarming than a sick dog wagging her tail when you step into the room? What more pleasing affirmation of your worth can you imagine – in your dog's eyes you are a beloved and revered king? It's enough to make your eyes well up.

Of course dogs bite people and rip their scalps and chew off their faces sometimes. Such viciousness, directed elsewhere, can be useful, in fact, once was, ten thousand years ago. Because of it dogs were immensely more important then than they are today. Why? A pack of snarling community dogs in a stone-age village helped terrified villagers beat off howling packs of wolves time and again, of that there can be no doubt. You must admit, though, that villages aren't besieged by ravenous wolves much anymore (thankfully), besides, today half of the ranging wolves that survive out in the free are ear-tagged and lug around radio transmitters on their necks thanks to game biologists who insist they are seeking to preserve wolves in their "wild" state. Cough, cough.

Dogs aren't much needed for village wolf-defense these days. Hence they've lost a lot of value.

No, it is definitely not the dog that we should love more than any other. It's just not.

Nor is it the cat, the hamster or the parakeet. Or the goldfish.

It's the COW, dearie.

I'm talking about good-old mooing Bossie the Cow, you know, the benevolent brute which gives us pure white milk with little frothy bubblets floating atop it and blesses us not only with delightful milk mustaches but with juicy-dripping filet mignons and sweet-scented cowhide leather coats as well. What animal does more?

Cows aren't romantic like, say, unicorns are, I admit; they hardly ever make hearts flutter. And yet they are such practical and useful brutes. Think about it. Do dogs give milk by the gallons? Hardly. Do parakeets dish out oh-so-tender filet mignons? Nope. Cows do. Of course Bossie also gives us cowpies and the sound of pee splatting on a flat rock – but this is unpleasant to mention and I shall defer discussing it till later, when I will be forced to do so. For the nonce I shall extol Bossie's virtues fulsomely.

Just one more thing so there's no mistake: We need to *appreciate* cows a lot more. That's my point. Without 'em we'd be in a peck of trouble. Not only that, they've changed our lives and left their stamp on our language's bones.

Cows roam everywhere in our imaginative literature, surely a sign of their importance. Didn't a cow once jump over the moon – and didn't the image of that giant-leap for bovinity you saw in your mind as a child impale you and jar your mouth agape, and give you a rush of pleasure? Go on; admit it, you, too, imagined that cow's prodigious vault in *your* mind's eye, didn't you? And it was wonderful, sheer wonderful, you'll have to admit. Heroic acts by cows are less common these days, of course. And with the decline of the family farm and the disappearance of cows into milk factories all over America, cows have gone dry in our pulpy as well as our slick magazines, by which I mean the fleeting literature that fades away unnoticed till it is completely forgotten by all but the wild-eyed or the nostalgic few – I'm talking about things like Life Magazine and the comic strips and comic books of the 1930's. You don't remember them? That's my point! You hardly ever think about cows, either.

You will surely acknowledge that stories of the American West have thrilled millions around the world for nigh on to a century. Maybe you even read the stuff. Zane Grey was a legendary western writer (Riders of the Purple Sage, Nevada, Robber's Roost and dozens more). Then there was Owen Wister (The Virginian, The Johnson County War, When the West Was Won) as well as Louis L'Amour (Showdown at Yellow Butte, High, Lonesome, The Trail to Seven Pines) and many other lesser known authors. The central figure in this genre of American literature was the cowboy. Please be reminded here that there would have been no cowboys without cows. There's no chicken-and-egg problem here at all: it's beyond dispute that the cow came before the boy.

Speaking of literature, weren't *cow*boys the heroes of our callow years of longing (and lusting) youth, too, especially at the movies, at least from the 1920's into the 1960's. And weren't those cowboys young males (mostly, anyway) who lassoed and bulldogged the resisting longhorn *cows* to ground? Sometimes – in the deprecating spirit of American humor – those men called cowboys were called cowpokes, cowpunchers and cowhands, but whatever the name the cow was there and they were true men – or men-to-be, which is pretty much the same thing. In England or Scotland or on the European mainland, those who herded cows were called cowherds (or the equivalent – e.g., Kuhhirt in German). Cowherd luckily never caught on here. Maybe it's because there is something wimpy about it. Can you imagine a cowherd riding a bull? Why, he'd fall off like Humpty Dumpty and crack his shell in pieces before the bull lunged out of the chute!

There were *cow*girls in those movies of the '30's, '40's and '50's, too, but they were real live *women*, as different as steak is from hamburger-helper when viewed side-by-side with their prim-and-proper contemporary movie heroines who traveled about in carriages and who, if they ever did climb on a horse and ride off, did so sidesaddle. Our cowgirl, by contrast, opened her legs and leapt upon her steed, holding it tightly between her grasping thighs, using them to exert firm control of the horse brute under her – be it even a rearing stallion – and making it go just where *she* wanted to go. Now *there* was a real woman, in charge, on top of things, even if we misnamed her cow*girl*.

There were even cowmen, though mostly we saw them as prosperous middle-aged fellows with gold chains draped over vests. Those vests failed to hide their beginning-to-bulge bellies that threatened any day soon to lap lewdly over their belts. And these guys formed associations, termed cowmen's associations, to protect their economic interests and their high station in society. They hired the gunslingers and burned the sheepherders out. Not an admirable bunch.

Curiously, there were no cowwomen, or almost none. Why? This is disturbing, and I ponder on the reason for it. Was it an early form of gender bias, perhaps? Or might it simply be that the tongue trips too clumsily over words with back-to-back w's in the middle? (Other than powwow, what example can you think of?) Three syllables are more cumbersome by far than two, by the way, and that might be a factor as well. Actually, one does on rare occasions see reference to cowwomen, but it is usually a bitching comment that raises the same query I do here: Why aren't there more cowwomen? One women's libber was deeply annoyed that a woman had to dress herself in cowboy boots, asking disdainfully why she couldn't get cowwomen's boots. At least she didn't have to purchase cowmen's boots.

When I was a half-grown kid trying to figure out what life was about, in Linton, in the mid 1950's, I became intimately familiar with cows, even though I grew up in town. The nicest thing (in my view at the time) about a small town was that a walk of 10 or 15 minutes in most any direction delivered you into the countryside. The fascinating countryside! To the west and south of Linton that countryside was fascinating in a dilapidated way – there were ruins of abandoned deep mines with their tipples caving in, barren meadows, spoiled creeks that still ran yellow-red with iron stains, and slag heaps 40 feet tall from the washing of the coal all those years ago, and disused railroad spurs. To the north were the stripper hills – the steam shovels of the 1920's had created those hills after it was discovered that digging the overburden off the coal was cheaper, faster and less dangerous than tunneling after the coal underground the way my Scottish grandfather did and hundreds of other Linton miners did. The stripper hills, whose irregular folds by chance formed the banks of Horseshoe Pond, Mink Pond, Rotten Egg, and Grand Canyon, among others, were perfect for hunting and trapping but worthless for anything else. No cows were to be found there either. It was to the northeast, just north of Jerry Brown's house on the edge of Linton, that there were grassy pastures, and cows.

I remember one of those pastures sharply, for I visited it a hundred times at least over several summers. In that pasture I discovered something utterly fascinating to my nubile mind, something I loved to watch far more than the still-new television. When I rode my bicycle to that pasture I usually parked it at Brown's house on 10th Street Northeast, and took him along if he was so inclined. The plot of ground in question was a few acres of slightly rising meadow through which a little brook trickled. Over the centuries freshets in the waterway had washed out some fairly deep cuts here and there, with banks a few feet high, and in the northwest of the pasture there was a shady grove of white oaks where the cows lay on hot summer days and chewed their cuds reflectively. When their four stomachs emptied and began growling, the dozen or so Guernsey brutes – brown-and-white dappled ladies with big pink udders – rose and wandered around the pasture, crunching the grass and the clover and creating, by their meanders, a wandering maze of foot-wide cow paths crisscrossing the verdant acres.

And everywhere the cows did go they left their piles of poop. We affectionately called their leavings cowpies because they resembled in their round outlines the circular consumables that came steaming from the oven. (On a cool morning, I observed, cowpies, fresh from a cow's rear end, gave off rising wisps of steam just as did an apple pie fresh from the oven. Maybe that's why the name cowpie seemed so appropriate.) Being kids, and therefore enjoying shocking people by saying something slightly indecent, we naturally laughed when we associated something revolting (cow poop) with a beloved food. In any case cowpies they were to us, though we were aware of competing terms for them, such as pasture patties, meadow muffins, and country pancakes. I hardly need to point out – it will have been noted already by the more astute readers among you – that these alternative amusing appellations likewise link cow dung with food.

It was to those cowpies we (if Brown was with me) made a beeline right after we ducked through the barbed wire fence at the edge of the pasture. Does this seem peculiar, reader, our seeking out cowpies? It does?

Not to me, and not to Jerry either. For what earthly reason did we do that?: That pasture was a living zoo of dung beetles, one of life's utterly fascinating creatures. Dung beetles needed dung, obviously, and the cows provided it in abundance. And watching dung beetles was just about the best free fun anywhere. I tell you that dung beetles live lives that are at one and the same time preposterous, amazing, hilarious, deadly earnest, ridiculous and useful. They are my favorite insects – butterflies and wild silkworm moths excepted.

Does it seem a head-scratcher to you, reader, that I, a former boy and now somewhat dignified but beginning-to-creak mature man declare that one of his favorite insects is a poop-scooping black beetle? If you are puzzled by this, I'll bet you have never in your life watched a pair of those dung ball drivers pile into their work.

It's unforgettable and amusing and thought-provoking at the same time. Bend over with me and have a look!

The pasture dung beetles (also known as tumblebugs) that Brown and I watched so avidly are shiny-black, spherical fellows the size of a dime, the female being larger than her mate. They have flattened heads and long, horny and spiny legs. Their walk may be best described as a scramble. But it is what they scramble after that rivets our attention: it is a ball of cow poop the size of a quarter, perfectly round, remarkable so, and we immediately scratch our heads and wonder how these little beetles learned how to make such a perfect sphere out of poop. For it is cow poop they use; somehow the curious couple of beetles use their heads (literally and figuratively) to fashion their orb out of one of the abundant cowpies.

Once their little poop bonbon is made, they set off with it, still as a couple, in a roughly straight line lickety-split on a radial from the cowpie, using mostly their hind legs to kick and push the yellow-brown orb forwards. The speed with which they move it surprises – several feet an hour at least. The pair works together, sometimes the male hangs on for dear life atop the ball while the female shoves their treasure forward.

At a critical moment he unbalances it all and helps tumble it forward; he sometimes being flung off in a crack-the-whip maneuver. Obstacles like clumps of grass or broken stones that loom in the way cause the excitable pair consternation; they abandon their treasure temporarily and start running around, distracted and discombobulated, but eventually a bypass is found around the hindrance. The pair leaves the impression of intense commitment and pertinacity. Eventually, satisfied they have pushed their load far enough, they use their front legs to dig a hole, in which they hide their ball. Before this operation is complete, the lady deposits an egg in the mass, which develops into a larva that grows to full size within the orb, eating out the heart of the thing, thriving on the nutrients left by the cow. Eventually the larva transforms into a pupa and, in the following spring or summer, out from their earthy caves spills the next generation of black tumblebugs to start the cycle again.

Although there is definitely cooperation between the lady and her smaller mate, their shenanigans sometimes resembled those of the keystone cops. There are pratfalls and stumbles; sometimes the ball maliciously rolls over its rider and pins him (or her) to the ground momentarily. On occasion it squirts away from its managers and rolls down a little incline. A panic attack ensues in the hearts of the beetles; they scramble over themselves, tangling up with one another while trying to go in opposite directions. Sometimes the ball gets stuck between a weed stem and the ground and they work like slaves to free it, pushing and pulling it from every angle.

Here's where Brown and I found malicious fun. With a thin sharp-pointed stick we impaled the ball in the ground. Talk about going wild! Try as mightily as they could, the frustrated beetles couldn't manage to move it, though they strained at it for an hour. Once when we did this they just tried to bury the ball where it was – but it wouldn't go down because it was stuck on the stick. They eventually abandoned this immovable ball, I suspect, though it was getting dark at the time and I had to go home for supper and didn't see the actual outcome.

There were other ways to drive them into a scrambling fit, the best of which was to steal their ball! Search and search they did, wildly and in obvious despair, driven to distraction, the poor things with their antennae quivering. They eventually gave the thing up for lost forever, and went in search of another cowpie to make a replacement.

In that pasture north of Brown's house you couldn't walk ten steps on a sunny June day without spotting a pair of laboring tumble bugs. They were everywhere and cowpies were everywhere, too – in fact you had to be careful where you put your foot because it was no fun at all to dip your new white sneakers up to their tops into a still-steaming freshly-deposited half-liquid cowpie. There are few feelings of disgust that can top that one.

Why were there so many cowpies and so many big black beetles tumbling around that pasture like pinballs in slow motion? It's because cows are so productive of manure – not only milk comes in abundance from cows, so does the residue out the adjacent end of the brute. You probably have never bothered to think about it, but a healthy dairy cow can produce 18,000 pounds of milk a year. If this makes you gasp, watch out, because the same animal can produce 28,000 pounds of manure in the same time interval. One cow!

Set a dozen cows rambling over a few acres of pasture with plenty of grass to chew and water to drink and before long the pasture is besotted with cowpies. What happens if those cowpies lay there undisturbed? The grass underneath is killed. Only slowly does it recover as the poop dries out; this may take weeks. The productivity of the pasture is reduced. That concentrated heap of manure is too rich to support plant life. It's an overabundance of nutrients. What is needed – you (a gifted problem solver) realize, is for that manure flop to be redistributed over the meadow, scattering the nutrient-rich manure so its benefits spread far more evenly, fertilizing more area and far more plants. That's exactly what farmers do (or used to do) if they have an excess of manure in their barnyards: scoop it into the manure spreader and fling with over the meadow with that implement. What would even be more better (you say to yourself as you pull your chin) is for those manure nutrients to be deposited directly underground, into the root field of the meadow plants. That would *really* be beneficial. Not even your modern farmer does *that*. The perceptive reader has now already begun to hear the trumpets of the cavalry as it rides to the rescue: Da Da Dahhhh Ta Dah! It is the super dung beetle! It does exactly what is needed – redistribute and bury the manure residue, for the benefit of everyone – even the kid who carelessly trips through the meadow in his white sneakers, oblivious of the camouflaged cowpies.

Thanks to the spectacle of dung beetles, cows and cowpies became part of my early life. I'm sure everyone over 40 or 50 has a similar (yet different) tale of how they were influenced by the cud-chewing bovine.

For sure no one will dispute that cows (in some form or other) have worked their ways deep into our language. You don't believe me? Holy Cow! I never thought you would say that! Are you saying that you've never called something a sacred cow? I have to confess that as a teenager I used to enjoy referring to my domineering sister as "Boss

Cow." And when our annoying and corpulent neighbor lady was out of earshot I declared loudly that she was a real cow. If she had known what I called her she would have had a cow. I certainly remember fondly the really pretty red-headed girl I once had a crush on: she won me over one day by making cow eyes at me.

Of course cows appear in many other forms. I am led to wonder if cows eat cowpeas, cowslip, cow parsnip and cow vetch? And do they get cow pox, or just transmit it? I know we all worry a lot these days about mad cow disease, which causes some of us to be cowed into not eating beef. Maybe we even cower in fear. Milk sickness – a pioneer disease caused by cows eating Virginia snakeroot in the dry fall time in the woods – caused their milk to be poisonous. Long ago, this cow-caused disease killed Nancy Hanks, Abraham Lincoln's mother. It sickened thousands of pioneers every fall in the Midwest.

There is so much more about cows. I've left out the breeds and their origins and genetic history, their domestication, and their multitude of uses. And I've not even said a word yet about oxen. In fact, I believe I could write about cows till … till … till the cows come home!

A Murder of Crows

Light thickens, and the crow makes wing to the rooky wood.

- Shakespeare, MacBeth, Act III, Scene 2

For some mysterious reason the children of our species (*Homo sapiens**) are fascinated by animals, love them, adore them. Sometimes it is a kitten, a cuddly wittle wabbit or maybe a dyed-yellow chick at Easter time, cheeping pitifully and evoking cries of "ohhhhhh" and "ouuuuuu." But it can as well be a snake, too, a bat, or even, as in the case of son Ian and daughter Heather in the 1980's, a little snapping turtle they dipped out of Wildcat Creek while we were canoeing. The diminutive pet snapper eventually died, not surprisingly, considering its sudden change of habitat and the rigors of being fondled, petted, and hugged nonstop from morn till night. Said turtle's demise caused copious sobs and loud lamentations. These were not extinguished until the little turtle's solemn burial the next day. This took place under a rock in the backyard of our place there on Platte Drive in Lafayette, Indiana. The death of "Snappy" had its uses. It caused the kids to *think* for the first time about death. They had seen the real thing with their very own eyes now, and held it in their hands, and they were devastated.

Homo sapiens (= wise man) is an egregious misnomer, by the way, as I have long since sadly concluded.

Death, they learned, is immediately followed by a sense of loss, sadness, and then by regrets: Maybe if they had fed Snappy better? Unanticipated but useful things sometimes come from having pets.

Thirty years earlier, in the mid-1950's, I myself had been afflicted by the same pet-o-mania as my kids had with their snapping turtle. I had my own series of pets, most of them, like Snappy, caught in the wild and maintained – for a mercifully short time in the view of Mom – in the far corner of the linoleum-floored kitchen at the back of our house on Second Street Northwest in Linton.

I had a raccoon for a pet for a short while. We had found it trying to nurse its car-struck dead mother on a country road. I never got the wild out of it. It had needle-sharp teeth and as it grew it became meaner and meaner and bit harder and harder. When it eventually got out of its cage and ran away – by that time its bites were drawing droplets of blood – I didn't miss it much; it never lived up to my expectations of a pet raccoon anyway.

I had several squirrels for pets, but the conditions under which I acquired them were not conducive to their living long. Splashing through the leaf-littered early spring woods with my buddies Dick Haseman and Jerry Brown, we would halt before a tree with a squirrel's nest, and take turns shinnying up, a club in our belt, and commence flailing at the nest. Most of them were empty and all we got for our efforts was skinned forearms and a sweaty forehead. Now and then there scampered out of the nest a half-grown squirrel, which we judiciously clubbed in the head with the idea of merely knocking it out. It never occurred to us that knocking out a squirrel with a club (or any animal, for that matter) was anything more than a harmless little bop in the head. Hadn't we watched hundreds of knockouts at the movies, where our overwhelmed hero, confronting a mob of desperadoes, was clubbed from behind and went down in a heap, only to wake up hours later, trussed to a chair by an endless girdle of rope. And when he opened his eyes didn't he just shake his head a couple of times, after which he was totally normal and ready to leap atop the bar to spring onto the evildoers and thereby save the maiden, who was about to be ravaged on the poker table in the back of the saloon? The nice thing about pet squirrels obtained in this way is that, knocked out, they didn't bite you with their rodent teeth that can easily slice through a stone-hard hickory nut. The regrettable thing about knocking them in the head to tame them was that they were almost always goofy and usually died within days of their capture.

There was a pet that I longed for even more, and which, at last I succeeded in obtaining: a crow, a real, big, cawing wing-flapping crow. No bird – at least in the American Midwest – is noisier and more raucous that the common crow. Every small town kid was familiar with crows and their rookeries and recognized them from their "songs" and all of us could imitate it with a raucous "caw, caw!" Every boy was familiar too with the little black swooshes they made against the evening sky when they migrated to their communal roosts.

Well, after Brown, Haseman and I gave up on squirrels, we decided to become the masters of pet crows, and imagined ourselves strutting around Linton with crows perched on our shoulders. One of us had discovered – I don't remember which it was – that you can find a crow's nest by being crafty, quiet and observant – if you look in the right place at the right time. I hope the reader knows that crows are normally gregarious, commonly trailing noisily around the surrounding countryside in gaggles and gangs. As they forage, they scatter everywhere, looking here for a road-killed possum to pluck at till a car comes along, or maybe finding there a spill of corn in the mud where the farmer had carelessly unloaded his crib. Crows, being jealous fellows like other birds, watch one another closely and are suspicious of one another. They learn early in their lives that 40 eyes are better than two, but only if they keep a sharp eye on those other crows and rush to share in the treasure they discover lest they devour it and leave you hungry.

But a mother crow is another bird indeed, for she is quiet and circumspect. She builds her nest – assisted by her mate and sometimes one of her earlier offspring, too. She usually puts it high in a tree, often in the crotch of the main trunk. There, in a two-foot wide nest of rough twigs cupping a softer center-nest of fine grass, she deposits her four or five blue or grey-mottled eggs, and incubates them till there emerges some of the ugliest, featherless chicks you ever saw. Responsible together with her husband for feeding these hideous waifs, she makes frequent forays into the countryside, visiting that fly-covered possum carcass or the spilled grain, carrying it back to regurgitate the repulsive mess into the yawning mouths of her babes. While free-ranging crows are notoriously loud, mother crow is just the opposite. As she approaches her nest from a foraging expedition, she flies low and silently among the trees, never calling attention to herself for fear, probably, of alerting a raccoon or a prowling blacksnake to the location of her babies.

That's how Brownie, Dick and I located promising crows' nests. Before the spring dawn rose purple and pink, we rode our bicycles to a woods somewhere out beyond Linton's city limits, hiding our bikes under some bushes at the edge of the road by a woods known to be a haunt of crows. We stole quietly into the woods and then separated, each of us taking station at different points across the woods. There we squatted, our backs against the trees, waiting and watching as dawn seeped silently like an ever brighter light into the air around us. Sooner or later, if we were lucky, we spotted a silent black form flying among the tree trunks and emerging into the open country beyond. This told us that there was indeed a crow's nest in the neighborhood. After some minutes, or even an hour, she came back, as silent as ever – even though other crows were cawing in the far distance. We watched as she disappeared into the woods, and noted the line she was taking, whereupon we changed position till we were closer to her still-unknown destination deeper in the woods. After some time, we saw her again depart the woods and then later enter again. This allowed us to better triangulate the spot from which she was coming and going. There, although the trees by that time of the year were partially leafed out, we spotted her big, twiggy nest, high above the wood's floor. When she flew off on her next foraging expedition, up the tree I shinnied, a pillowcase hanging from my belt. Forty feet up, I plucked those ugly featherless little lumps of flesh with their tiny imperfect quills just beginning to show. One by one I slipped them carefully into the sack. Then quickly down the tree I scraped and slipped, before the mother crow returned, and hurried away home with the others – fearful of the beak and the flogging wings of the wrathful mother till I escaped the still dim woods. Dick and Brownie had theirs in the bag, too, and we soon parted ways for home.

Baby crows are helpless. Still blind at the time we took them, they were soon at home in the rag-lined shoebox I placed in the kitchen corner by the register. The shoebox itself was kept on a spread of newspapers – for good purpose. When the little lumpy things pooped, they backed themselves up till they encountered the wall of the box, whereupon they raised their rumps, puckered up and then spurted their lump of doodoo over the side, where it landed harmlessly but with a splat on yesterday's Linton Daily Citizen spread under their box as a poop catcher.

Feeding the still-blind, unfledged uglies was literally child's play. All I had to do was lean my face over the shoebox and make a raspy cawing sound. Up the drowsing things would bounce, raising their heads like jacks-in-the-box to the limit of their height and spreading their jaws till all I could see were the yellow waving diamond shapes of their maws as they jockeyed for the favor of some morsel from their mother – me. The reader should understand that because I acquired the little crowlets before their eyes opened, the first thing they saw when they did finally open them was me, a grinning 12-year old human. I actually didn't realize it myself, but I was the only mother they ever really knew, and they remained ever comfortable and trusting in my presence.

Thanks to being fed regular meals of hunks of bread dipped in milk, or night-crawlers I had picked up on the sidewalk after the latest thunderstorm, my little charges waxed fat and ever bigger. Before long the sharp-eyed fellows got their black fledging and soon began hopping up on the rim of their shoebox to follow me or Mom with their alert eyes as we moved about the kitchen.

Mom eventually persuaded me that I didn't need *three* crows, that one would do, and so I gave the others away to friends. I kept the biggest, shiniest one, whose dark brown eyes and black legs and beak blended perfectly with the purple-black of his (or was it her?)

magnificent feathers. I called him Blackie, and was soon strutting around the neighborhood with him perched on my shoulder. He soon began learning to fly, and this led me to tie a loop of kite string around his ankle, and secure the other end of a twenty foot strand to a stick the length of a walking cane. He soon learned that flying has its limitations – it hurt when he came to the end of his tether and the weight of the stick jerked him to a stop in mid-air. In any case he soon adapted and accepted that any flights he made had to be shorter than 20 feet.

Dellie and Charlie Brock enjoyed my crow as much as I did, Dellie frequently declaring that it was a "right-smart" fine-looking bird. It was indeed by mid-summer nearly a foot long and weighed the better part of a pound. Charlie seemed a bit troubled that it couldn't talk, and wasn't particularly impressed that Blackie would respond to me when I said "caw" merely by throwing open its mouth in preparation to receive food. I think he said to himself "That's nothing!" – but he liked me too much to say it because it might hurt my feelings.

"When I was a boy," he said, "Dicky Parker down the pike from us had a crow and he split its tongue. After that it would talk and say all kinds of things, like 'Hello, Dicky!' and 'Feed me, feed me!' and other such."

This comment made me think that Charlie was disappointed in Blackie, and this bothered me. As a consequence I actually thought about splitting the poor bird's tongue, but I didn't know how to go about it, and so I kept putting the operation off till I figured out how to do it. Although I would never have admitted it then, I thought the operation to be a brutal one – but my friends would have called me a sissy if I admitted that – and that's why I never did.

By the time that spring was over and summer began to open its blossoms, I kept Blackie – at Mom's insistence – in the backyard. He sat on a pole-perch I had pounded into the ground by the sidewalk under the red maple tree. The crossbar on which Blackie sat was at about 5 feet – about as high as me at the time. I kept the far end of his tether string tied to the pole, just in case Blackie should decide to join a passing flock of crows some day. As I shoved my way through the screen door out of the house, Blackie, delighted, probably because of the prospect of a tidbit of food, which I usually had for him, would fly from his perch and alight like a bundle of night on my shoulder. There he would sit, making a sort of purring sound or chuckling sound, and now and then taking my earlobe in his beak, not enough to hurt, mind you, but enough to get my attention. Sometimes I would hold up my right hand and he would crawl on my wrist and we would walk to his perch, he leaning forward and staring me in the eye all the while, beseeching something to eat.

I was a sucker for that crow, for whom I had real affection. Alas, too much affection can be bad for a person and bad for a crow, too, as I discovered. One day, walking past his perch with my friend

Jimmy Schmitt, we stopped so I could show off Blackie, which Jimmy had never seen. From the time he was a blind half-feathered lump, Blackie had responded to my "Caw!" by opening his beak wide in the expectation of food.

"Caw!" I croaked. Blackie opened his beak wide.

"I don't have anything to give him," I said.

"How about these?" Jimmy said, as he pulled a packet of multicolored M&M's out of his pocket.

"Sure, why not? I don't know why he wouldn't like M&M's."

Well, I dropped an M&M into Blackie's maw, and he seemed to be delighted, though he may have been just as pleased had it been a piece of gravel. Soon Jimmy asked if he could try it.

He said "Caw!" Blackie opened wide. In plopped an M&M. Jimmy was delighted and so was I. My little performer was performing.

"Can I try it again?"

"Sure," I said. "Why not?"

To make a long story short, Blackie soon got into the spirit of the thing, hopping around and begging for more, opening his beak wide and cawing and acting silly and delightful. Every time he hopped or reared back open-mouthed he got another M&M. Soon my buddy and I discovered that if we threw an M&M into the air close to his head, Blackie, nimble as he was, could catch it.

All three of us were having a barrel of fun.

Eventually, we ran out of M&M's and Jimmy had to go home anyway. It was getting dark by that time, and so I went into the house to have supper before watching Uncle Milty or Ted Mack's Amateur Hour on our big new 17 inch black and white TV.

The following morning, still half asleep and rubbing the sleep out of my eyes, I pushed out the back door of the kitchen to renew my friendship with Blackie; I found a heap of black feathers lying stiff, cold and dead in the dewy grass. By engorging him with chocolate candies, I had given him a lethal case of hyperglycemic shock, and so caused his demise. M&M's and crows are not meant for one another.

Another pet, another death, another sense of loss, with sadness and regrets. I wandered around for days after that in a mood as black as a crow's wing. That crow had made a deep impression on me.

Crows have fascinated people far into the misty past. There's good reason for that. Not only are they big (a foot long) black, loud birds, they are extremely intelligent. They are easily as smart as other animals noted for being highly intelligent; and their brains are as large relative to their bodies as those of our smart near-relatives, the chimpanzees, are to theirs. Given a piece of wire, a crow has been seen to bend the wire into a hook and use it to snag bits of food outside its cage.

Long ago, the Greek Aesop was an admirer of crows. He composed his fable of the crow and the pitcher – a tribute to the bird.

A crow, he said, dying of thirst, came upon a pitcher. In the pitcher there was a little water but it was too far down for the crow to reach as he stood on the rim. Spying a nearby pebble, he hopped to it and picked it up in his beak. Hopping back to the pitcher, he dropped the pebble in. This he did again and again, until, at last, the water rose high enough for him to reach.

The moral of the story is that little by little does the trick. Persistence and imagination can solve seemingly impossible problems. The crow had both.

Like one other intelligent animal, the aforementioned *Homo sapiens* (cough, cough), the crow can be vain to the point of absurdity, and as a result he estimates his talents far above their real worth. Aesop made fun of such people (and crows) in another of his fables. It seems a crow was sitting in the top of a tree with a hunk of cheese in his beak. A passing fox, spotting the crow with the mouth-watering chunk of cheese, called to him in admiring terms, telling him how black and beautiful he was and imploring him to sing a song. The crow, flattered and vain, opened his beak to warble, but could only manage to make some coarse squawks and caws. As he attempted to sing, out fell the hunk of cheese directly into the waiting maw of the fox, which trotted happily away.

One should, Aesop told us, know our own limitations.

Though a minor player in this long ramble of words, the crow of folklore and actual experience has impressed us and worked its way into our lives and speech, sometimes in subtle ways. Something that is really black is as black as a crow, or as a crow's wing. This reminds me that the use of birds in the culinary arts date far back into antiquity. Henry the Eighth, for example, enjoyed the occasional hummingbird pie, and we all remember hearing about the legendary four and twenty blackbirds baked in a pie. But note also that if we are truly humbled we are forced to eat crow. I remember the small town politics of Linton of the 1950's, where, after the election results were all counted, there was a crow supper. The victors got public opportunity to crow over their defeated opponents, while watching those humbled folk eat crow, not, please note, blackbirds. Why did they not say "eat blue jay" or "eat owl?" For some reason the crow was chosen as the archetype of a repulsive or abominable meal. Maybe it is because they are black and because human beings rarely eat anything that is black. Perhaps more likely, the rejection of crow as food comes from the crow's habit of eating carrion. And of plucking out the eyes of the newly dead. The raven, the first cousin of the crow, has long since become associated with graveyards and death.

But crows are there in our language for other reasons, nearly all of them negative. One of the oddities of crows is their curious bipedal locomotion. Unlike a lot of birds, they not only walk – in a kind of waddling way – but they also hop, feet parallel, and they can do so at surprising speed, leaving tracks. A person whose years have caught up with him (or her) acquires crow's feet – intersecting dark lines around the eyes like the tracks of crows in the dust.

If birds threaten our garden, poking holes in the ripening tomatoes and puncturing the sweet corn, what measure do we take to ward it off? – We put up a scarecrow. Who ever heard of a scarecowbird or a scarerobin, anyway? Nobody. The crow, by implication, is an evilest crop-stealing bird.

Crows have tight-knit families, which assemble into large flocks in the fall and winter. Whenever a murder of crows – a strange term for a group of birds, isn't it? – is foraging in an area, one of them always perches high in a tree, keeping lookout. He caws his warning loudly if danger – in the form of a fox or a hunter – looms. And so it was that long ago the lookout on ships at sea took station in a barrel high on the mainmast, shouting a warning when other ships, rocky breakers or icebergs loomed   his high perch was of course called the crow's nest.

Since the time of the Greeks we have known that the shortest distance between two points in a straight line, but seldom could we save time and effort by taking it. Rare was the road that didn't curve over hill and dale and around the mountain. People have envied birds the miracle of flight from time immemorial. Still today, when they want to describe the most direct route from point A to point B, they preface their estimate saying "as a crow flies …"

Tiring now of this essay, I shall settle back into my easy chair with a relaxing drink. I'll believe I'll make it a bourbon:

"Reach down that bottle out of the cabinet for me, please. No, no, *not* that one, not the Wild Turkey, that's too harsh for my taste. Take down the one beside it, see it there, the one with the black bird on the label. That's it, that's it, my favorite, ahhhh …Old Crow."

I guess not everything is bad about crows.

"An old crow says to his son,
We crows have a saying:
Trust a man until he bends
To pick up a stone."

Stubborn as a Mule

I was six or seven years old when I first saw a mule. It was in the summer of 1948 or 1949, in the alley behind our house on Second Street Northwest, in Linton. Actually, there were *two* mules. To my little-kid eyes they were like horses, though somehow different. I was struck by their ears, big rabbity ones that pointed toward the sky like corn leaves. Their eyes were special, too, big and glistening brown, with long lashes. They turned their heads and looked around, following me in such a curious, interested way that I knew at once they were smart. They were gray, tall, and rangy, altogether imposing. Out of respect, or good sense, I made sure not to get too close to them. To describe them as *big* isn't useful, since to me, at that age, everything was big.

In any case it was the work the mules were doing and the striking appearance of the man they were with that made my eyes widen.

They were pulling an old-fashioned four-wheeled farm wagon, a grey unpainted wooden box on tall wooden-spoked wheels, and it was heading up the cinder-strewn alley behind our house. On the bench at the front sat a man like a proud, benevolent captain. He smiled at me as he shouted "whoa" to the mules. At that age my standards of cleanliness weren't very well developed, but even so he was obviously a dirty and greasy guy wearing clothes that would qualify for the rag bag. He sported a bushy, unkempt beard that curled about his grimy beaming face like a swirling storm cloud. Nobody wore beards in those days (except when a town had its Centennial), so whiskers set the man apart. He seemed, with his crooked chewing-tobacco-stained teeth, to be remarkably cheery.

"How dee do boy?" he said, positively beaming.

"Fine," I replied. "How do you do, Mister?"

"Is yer mother to home?"

I admitted she was, which seemed to please him greatly, for his smiling face lighted up further, as if I had given him a fine present.

"Thank ye, son!" he burbled, hopping down off his seat and making his way unhurriedly toward the back door. After a brief chat with Mother – during which he held his stained cloth cap deferentially in his hand while Mother stood defensively, half behind the partly opened screen door. She seemed ready to slam and lock it instantly against this hobo-like fellow if danger threatened. He soon came shambling back, whistling, and obviously pleased. He sprang back on his seat, called to the mules, which backed the wagon twenty feet or so, stopping it at the rear wall of our family coal house and privy.

I should explain that in those days the folks who lived on our street didn't yet have indoor plumbing. Calls of nature required you to make a trip to the outhouse, sometimes carrying a granite-ware chamber pot filled the night before. Our family facility was a single-holer with a door whose knob was black porcelain. I remember it because on many a frosty January day that porcelain knob gave my fingers an icy bite.

The thing about privies was that they eventually filled up with, uh, uh, let's call it "residue." At some point there was no option but to clean out the accumulated .... I guess I'll have to call it by its four-letter Anglo-Saxon word .... poop.

The alley behind our house was dotted with outhouses, eight of them in all (none of them built of brick, incidentally), one behind each house, all of which faced Second Street. Walking down the alley on a windless summer day meant holding your nose (or at least your breath) when you passed a privy needing sanitary services. Usually at least one of them did.

Cleaning out privies wasn't a job for the faint-hearted, and certainly not one that ordinary folks cared to do. What do you do with the stuff, anyway? And so when I watched the cheerful grimy fellow hop down again from his perch on the wagon and raise the hinged gate at the base of our outhouse, it finally dawned on me what he was about. He was a professional privy cleaner, and his vehicle was one of those notorious honey wagons. True, it wasn't a dignified occupation, but the demand for it was steady. And the pay was good. Mom gave him five dollars for undertaking the odious task.

I watched, at a distance, grimacing, as he dug out the residue with a long-handled shovel, tossing shovel-load after shovel-load of the disgusting stuff over the wooden wall into the bed of the wagon, on which it landed with a liquid plop. All the while the guy whistled and hummed with a pipe clenched between his teeth. He stopped from time to time to relight the pipe with a big kitchen match. Though I was a mere wee tyke, and spent part of the time circling the mules to see them at different angles, I distinctly remember wondering how a man doing such a disgusting job could be so darned happy. For me, at six or seven, the world was still filled with wonders.

When his poop-shoveling was done, he pitched several shovels of quicklime into the pit, and scattered more of it on the ground on the lip of the pit to soak up stuff that had spilled from his shovel. Then, still whistling, he closed up the hinged gate of the privy and hopped back on his seat on the wagon. He paused for a moment to take a nip from a bottle in a brown paper bag he kept on the seat. After a pleased sigh and a laugh, he took the reins in his hand, flicked them over the backs of the mules while making a clucking sound with his tongue, whereupon the mules and wagon went crunching on up the alley.

Moments later, back at my play – I was tossing a rubber ball against the side of the garage – I was startled by a loud braying coming from up the way. Running out to the alley I soon saw the cause of it. The honey wagon had stopped behind old Miss Pigg's house, and one of the mules had gotten annoyed at something, maybe it was the barking of a dog. There it stood, ears laid back on its neck, nose pointed at the sky, its lips peeled back to reveal long rows of teeth, emitting a series of resounding Whinee-Ahh-Ahh-Ahh! Whinee-Ahh-Ahh-Ahh! I didn't know whether it was a call of protest or a declaration of pride or what, but I was deeply impressed by its loudness. The neighbors were impressed too, for several of them came out their back doors to see what was the matter.

A mule is the offspring of a horse mare and a donkey jack (or stallion). With such parents, it isn't any wonder that the mule starts off life with a bad reputation. Mules come in all shapes and sizes, from miniature fellows 36 inches at the withers to draft monsters nearly 6 feet high. The size depends upon what the breeder chooses for parents. Mules come in nearly all the colors that horses do, from drab gray to brown and tan; some even have spotted patterns like pinto horses. One thing mules have in common is that they are all sterile. Maybe that's why they bray so miserably.

People love animals, often irrationally, and the mule is no exception. In addition to being interesting, mules proved *useful* in remarkable ways, and that was the real reason they became such a part of American life.

The first American to discover their usefulness was a soldier and a Virginia planter who had distinguished himself in a few other ways. His name: George Washington. Like other gentlemen farmers of his day, George was always on the lookout for ways to improve his farming operation. He heard about a fine new type of draft animal that had appeared in Spain, the offspring of a jack stallion and a horse mare. Thanks to George's reputation and connections, he soon wrangled the gift of a big jack from King Charles III of Spain. That was in 1785. After uniting his jack with a promising mare, he soon was the godfather of the first mule foal born in the new United States. By the time he died, George was the proud owner of 58 mules working his fields and drawing his wagons. Soon other farmers were imitating George and breeding mules on their own plantations. Mules quickly became the most popular draft animals in the growing nation and weren't supplanted in that role till the invention of the farm tractor in the early 20th Century.

Why were mules so useful? Because they are tougher and smarter than horses. You can ride a horse to death, but never a mule. When a mule senses he is working too hard and getting overheated, he slows down or even stops. No amount of shouting, cajoling or even beating can force him to go on doing what he knows is bad for him. He knows better than you do, and he knows it. Out of this sense of self-preservation grows his reputation for stubbornness. Actually, it's not stubbornness, but good sense. Horses will carelessly founder themselves and get the bloats and a bellyache, in other words, eat themselves sick. Mules won't. They eat what they need, then quit. That's why we say that someone eats like a horse, never that he eats like a mule. In our overweight age we need more of the latter and less of the former.

Unlike horses, mules rarely have hoof problems. Maybe that's because they have small, boxy feet, and are surefooted and careful where they step. In most other ways they are simply hardier and tougher. Veterinary costs for horses are far greater than those for mules. Mules work longer and live longer, too.

Mules are far more sensible than horses. If a horse gets tangled up in a barbed wire fence, he is liable to panic and tear wildly away, injuring himself in the process. A mule in the same situation remains cool and calm and tries to figure out how to extricate himself. If he can't solve the problem he will just wait till human help shows up. Mules are awfully smart. Clarence Calvert, who worked with his mules, Ike and George, as a kid seventy years ago, said that you had to take special precautions to keep the mules from getting into the next pasture. After watching you open and close a gate, Ike and George quickly figured out how to do it themselves. They would wait until you left, and then quickly find their way into the next field. They probably thought that the grass was greener over there.

All of these positive mule traits result from something scientists call hybrid vigor. The offspring of distantly-related but interbreedable animals or plants have vigor that neither of the parents possesses. It was the vigor of mules that made them beloved by Americans who needed animal power. And so they became the favorite working beasts on countless thousands of farms and highways of early America, right up till the tractor and the automobile age started a century ago.

Year after year mules pulled plows and mowing machines across a million American fields. And they drew countless dray wagons along the primitive highways of the growing nation. Until the Civil War, the majority of Americans lived on farms, and all those folks knew mules, if not first-hand on their own farms, then from their neighbors or from the roads that passed by their houses. Mules provided the power needed to pull enormous loads such as canal boats. Perhaps most famous were the twenty mule teams that pulled loads of borax across the desert to the rail head. It's interesting that Republican Ronald Regan, host of the popular 1950's TV show "Death Valley Days" had his name associated with a mule team that did work worthy of elephants. Despite the

fortune that Regan made on the backs of mules, he opted politically for the elephant instead.

The mule worked not only above ground, but underground, too. Coal mines in Pennsylvania and in the Midwest owed everything to the power of the mule. The mine mules were kept in underground stables, which saved the miners from having to coax them into and out of the mine elevator every day, a tricky operation at best. The little mules dragged the ponderous loaded coal cars from the coal face to the pit bottom, a notoriously dangerous operation – for the mule drivers, that is, who often lost their lives when they were run over or squashed between the pit timbering and the tunnel wall.

And so the mule worked its way into our American consciousness and language. It's not by chance that the mascot of the military academy at West Point is the Army mule. One of the most famous fighter units of World War I was the Kicking Mule Squadron, which distinguished itself over the skies of France. The squadron name carried a message: "We'll hit you hard, and we're smart! Watch out!" Quentin Roosevelt, son of former President Theodore Roosevelt, a Kicking Mule pilot, lost his life when he was shot down behind enemy lines on July 14, 1918. Frances the Talking Mule was a popular movie star in the 1950's. Frances was the companion, confidant and foil of Donald O'Connor in a series of comedy movies like Frances Goes to West Point. Frances invariably proved smarter than his human partner. Of course the symbol of the modern Democrat Party is the mule, and a lot of folks think it is a positive one.

Mule traits naturally came to be identified with human ones, that is, with our friends and neighbors. Someone who steadfastly refuses to change his mind is as stubborn as a mule, a phrase calling to mind the recalcitrant mule who simply sits down on its hindquarters and refuses to budge. A person who refuses to do something despite much urging balks like a mule. A loutish person who shouts in public brays like a mule. A man or woman who works steadily, dependably and hard, works like a mule. A person who transports illegal drugs is referred to in the trade (and by the police) as a mule. Someone who is taken advantage of by others is ridden like a mule. A person with a big toothy grin looks like a mule eating briars – the smart creature peels back his lips to keep from getting pricked. Anything that packs a powerful wallop and hits us unexpectedly kicks like a mule. Moonshine distilled in illegal stills and consumed without the mellowing aging process that also gave it color was referred to as "white mule," a once common alternative to "white lightning."

I'm tired of this essay now and so I refuse to write any more. I hope you don't think I'm being mulish.

www.ingramcontent.com/pod-product-compliance
Lightning Source LLC
Chambersburg PA
CBHW031252090426
42742CB00007B/425